GUARDIAN
OF THE STREETS

GUARDIAN
OF THE STREETS

JAMES COOK MBE
MY STORY

WITH MELANIE LLOYD

First published by Pitch Publishing, 2019

Pitch Publishing
A2 Yeoman Gate
Yeoman Way
Worthing
Sussex
BN13 3QZ
www.pitchpublishing.co.uk
info@pitchpublishing.co.uk

© 2019, James Cook with Melanie Lloyd

Every effort has been made to trace the copyright.
Any oversight will be rectified in future editions at the
earliest opportunity by the publisher.

All rights reserved. No part of this book may be reproduced,
sold or utilised in any form or transmitted in any form or by
any means, electronic or mechanical, including photocopying,
recording or by any information storage and retrieval system,
without prior permission in writing from the Publisher.

A CIP catalogue record is available for this book
from the British Library.

ISBN 978-1-78531-491-9

Typesetting and origination by Pitch Publishing
Printed and bound in India by Replika Press Pvt. Ltd.

CONTENTS

Acknowledgements 9
Introduction by Melanie Lloyd 11
Jamaica 17
London 27
Sporting Life 45
Boxing Beginnings 50
Carmen 62
The Grafter 75
The Professional 80
Billy Wynter 83
Darkie Smith 112
Harry Holland 129
Mickey Duff 152
The Boxing Coach 172
The Pedro Youth Club 196
The London Ex Boxers Association 221
The Secret Millionaire 234
From Rice and Peas to Your Majesty, Please 240
The Police 246
The Spirit of the Street 257
Final Reflections from the Champ 266

This book is dedicated to

my granny, my mum,
my Auntie Lovely
and Carmen.

ACKNOWLEDGEMENTS

There have been so many fantastic people in my life who have all helped me in so many ways to become the man I am today. I would have really loved to mention each and every one of them in this book. But, if I had done that, I would have had to ask Melanie if we could write another volume. So I would like to take this opportunity to mention all the names listed here, and I want to say to everybody who has supported me and who has been there with me that I thank you all from the bottom of my heart:

Jarvis Astaire, Dilley Williamson, Scott Ewing, Donté Clark OBE, Philip Sharkey, Sylvester Mittee, Derek Rowe, Dave Winkworth, Johnny Gallagher of J.J. Construction Limited, Mickey Collier, Jenny Levy, Olivier John Baptiste, Tomasz Krawczyk, S.S. Social Limited, Melvin and Babs, Gilbert and Patricia Anderson, Harold Alderman MBE, Everton, Mickey Helliet, Jay at Regal Pharmacy, Tony and Martin Bowers, Charlz Albert, Terry O'Connor, Wendy Smith, Adam Taylor, Addy and Ian Wilson from Everlast, Cecil Ross and Joey Moore. I would also like to give a special mention to a young lady who is six years old named Faye Marie.

Last but not least, thank you to my beautiful daughter, Lisa Cook, for helping Melanie with so many of the photographs. We honestly don't know what we would have done without her.

INTRODUCTION
by MELANIE LLOYD

WALKING around the streets of Lower Clapton in Hackney with James Cook MBE is an uplifting experience indeed. James seems to know everybody, and everybody seems to know James. Whether they be male or female, young or old, black, white or brown, huge smiles and vibrant greetings are enthusiastically exchanged with passers-by wherever he goes. In fact, the high esteem that James commands from within his local community is so apparent that you could almost reach out and touch it. They say that true respect has to be earned, and James has spent the best part of the past 60 years putting in the hard graft, although he will tell you that it has all been a labour of love.

James Cook was born in Jamaica in 1959 and, when he was still a baby, his parents entrusted him to the care of his grandparents so that they could travel to England in search of a better life for their family. When he was nine years old, James's mother travelled to Jamaica to collect her firstborn son and bring him home. The sunny days of a childhood spent climbing trees and playing cricket were replaced with an adolescence roaming the bleak and inhospitable streets of south-east London, the labyrinth of walkways on the North Peckham Estate often providing a handy escape route from the police or the local skinheads.

James was a teenager when he first discovered boxing, and the noble art has remained at the centre of his existence ever since. He started working with the youth when he was still an amateur boxer and little more than a boy himself, and the enjoyment he derives from making people smile and spreading happiness and peace is as strong in his heart now as it ever was. When he was 17 years old, he moved to Hackney, where he still lives today with his wife, Carmen, who was his childhood sweetheart back in Jamaica.

James spent 12 years in the professional boxing ring, and he was the type of fighter who learned very quickly to expect no special favours from the establishment. Against the odds, he captured the British and European super-middleweight titles. All the while he was exchanging blows in the toughest of sports, he never lost his focus on a very different kind of battle, the struggle against the crime, deprivation and delinquency that runs riot in our inner-city areas. When James wasn't pounding the streets doing his roadwork, he was striding the pavements as an outreach worker, his main objective being to get the local youth involved in sport, education, employment and an altogether more positive way of life.

When the time came for James to hang up his own gloves for good, he decided to become a trainer so that he could pass

INTRODUCTION

on the knowledge he had gained to help other fighters, fighters like he had been, fighters who were written off as having no chance. He relished the thrill of seeing many of his pugilistic pupils winning titles, but he also took an interest in their personal lives, and the loyalty that James engendered in the hearts of many of the fighters he trained remains evident to this day. Several of those boxers who passed through his most capable hands are still by his side, supporting him in his youth work in any way that they can.

In 2003, due to a lack of funds, the local council made the decision to shut down the Pedro Youth Club, which is situated just around the corner from where James lives. The Pedro was then, and still remains, the only youth club nestled between three colossal housing estates in an area that the *Daily Telegraph* once described as being 'more dangerous than Soweto'. On the day the council turned up to close the doors of the Pedro for good, James entered the building and took charge of the official documents. He made some phone calls and rapidly set up a management committee, thereby ensuring that this most important place would be allowed to carry on serving the community as it had been doing since 1929.

James is still the driving force at the Pedro, but he is quick to acknowledge all the dedicated people who work with him on a voluntary basis to ensure the club continues to thrive. He is also eternally grateful to the silent wall of individuals who slip him a cheque or an envelope of cash on a regular basis, many of whom approach him on the quiet at the London Ex

Boxers Association, where James has become a highly regarded goodwill ambassador.

In 2007, James received the MBE for services to youth justice in Hackney, and he fell in love with the Queen in the process. In some ways, it could be said that he has become a victim of his own success. Since he was named in the Honours List, the demands on his time have become endless. It is not unusual for James to receive 150 messages in one day and he does his best to respond to them all, especially when there is a hint that some desperately needed donations may be on the horizon. The Pedro receives no financial contribution from the government and, without the kindness of friends and strangers alike, the club would be unable to continue functioning.

In the meantime, James Cook continues to cut a formidable figure as he strolls down the road dressed in his street garb, overseeing all of the action that is going down on his manor. Sometimes, he looks quite stern as he exchanges banter with the youths that benefit from his care and devotion, but he seldom manages to keep a straight face for long. When his features transpose into the sunniest of smiles, he puts one in mind of an urban warrior who is on the side of everything that is right. To the young people he looks out for, James is their guardian angel. In their lives, which in many cases are destined to be uncertain and ever-changing, they know that James Cook is always there for them, always dependable, always the same.

The first time I ever interviewed James was over 20 years ago, when he was kind enough to take part in my first volume

INTRODUCTION

of *Sweet Fighting Man*. I can still remember that wet and wintery Sunday afternoon when he picked me up from the steps of York Hall in Bethnal Green. He took me back to his warm and comfortable home, where Carmen had rustled up a fantastic lunch, and I will never forget how she welcomed me in as if I was the most important visitor who had ever stepped across her threshold.

James was my first ever Caribbean boxer and, in my introduction to his chapter, I wrote about how his 'strong Jamaican accent remained softly soothing'. My second volume of *Sweet Fighting Man* came out just as James was about to receive his MBE, so he had 'The Last Word' in that book. That was when he told me in no uncertain terms, 'Mel, from now on, I want to be in every single book you ever *write!*' It certainly seems to have worked out that way, because James provided the foreword for *Ring of Truth*, the final part of the *Sweet Fighting Man* trilogy, and now I have had the honour and privilege of working with him on his autobiography.

Over the years, James has proved to be an excellent friend, and I have often benefited from his sound advice and solid wisdom. I still find his strong Jamaican accent softly soothing and, what is more, having made approximately 40 hours of recordings with James for this book, I can't help noticing that I have picked up a slight Caribbean lilt myself!

To my mind, one of the wonders of this world is the fact that, no matter how bad things get, there are always those special people who are willing to give so much of themselves in order to help others, people who spread light where there is darkness, compassion where there is destitution, warmth where there is need. The Pedro Youth Club is the beating heart of the Lower Clapton community. Some of the parents who take their children there nowadays used to go to the club when they were youngsters themselves, and they never forgot the strong and positive influence that James had on their lives. The Pedro Youth Club truly is an oasis of hope, and long may it live on so that future generations are able to reap the invaluable benefits that it provides. God bless you, James Cook MBE, and everything that you stand for.

JAMAICA

I WAS born on 17 May 1959 in a place called Runaway Bay in Saint Ann Parish, Jamaica. I don't think I was born in a hospital. To be honest, it is not something that I ever asked my mum about, but I'm pretty sure that I was born at home. There was a lady who was the local midwife in our area and, believe it or not, I ended up marrying her granddaughter, who is named Carmen. So, as far as I know, Carmen's granny was the lady who delivered me into this world.

When I was a small baby, my mum and dad left me in the care of my grandparents, because those were the days when a lot of Jamaican people were coming to England to find work. So, until I was nine years old, Jamaica was my home. Our place was just a normal house on top of a hill, and there was me, my granny and my grandad, my Uncle Frank, my Auntie Gloria, who we called Auntie Lovely, and my cousin, Wesley, who was great fun. We were always out playing together and getting up to stuff.

Uncle Frank was my mum's brother and he was about five years older than me and Wesley, so he was the one who we wanted to be like because he was the older one. So, when I was growing up, it used to be mainly me, Wesley and Uncle Frank who would be together. Anything Uncle Frank would do, me and Wesley would want to follow, and there were times when Uncle Frank led us into trouble. He used to get us to do his dirty work, and then me and Wesley would usually get the blame for it.

At mealtimes, one of things that me and Wesley used to do was leave the best bit, the chicken or the swordfish or whatever we were eating, until it was the last thing on our plates. We would eat all the rice and things like that, and we'd leave the nicest bit until the end. But, if we weren't quick enough, Uncle Frank would come along and he would grab our bit of chicken or fish, and it would be gone. So we soon learned to wolf down the best bits first. It was survival of the fittest in many ways. But we all had a lot of fun together and I think it was from my Uncle Frank that I got the idea I wanted to be a motor mechanic, because he was interested in cars and he used to bring cars home.

In the next house along from ours, there were six kids around the same age as me and Wesley. There were two girls named Carmen and Sonia, and there were four boys named Carlton, Lenbert, Everoy and Danny. Me and Wesley used to go out with them and we all used to do things together. Carmen and I used to be together quite a lot. She was very pretty and I liked her very much. We always used to ride this little donkey called Daisy together. I used to put Carmen in front of me, and I would be holding her from behind. We could see each other's houses and we could see what each other was doing, and Carmen was definitely my childhood sweetheart.

My granny was great. The years that I spent living with her were good times. I was her first grandson and Wesley was her second, and I still remember certain things she used to teach us and the words she used to say to me. She used to tell me, 'What's yours is yours. What you pay for is yours. When you die, they are not going to bury you with all your money and the things that you have. You can't take any of that with you.' From a very early age, granny used to teach us respect and manners. You couldn't go down the road and pass one of her friends and not say hello because, if that friend ever came back and told our granny 'I passed your grandson down the road and he didn't say hello to me,' trust me, granny would be waiting for you when you got home. She would tell you off, but she wasn't the sort of granny who would bully you or beat you.

My grandad was okay. Grandad was grandad. He was just there. Grandad would go out and pick his fruit and do his farming. Grandad was like my dad, very placid, very quiet. Granny was in charge. Anything granny said, grandad would go along with it. Sometimes our grandad would look at us and nod his head as if to give us a hint and say, 'If you don't behave, your granny is coming.' But grandad was all right.

My upbringing was quite strict, in the sense that I couldn't have gone off and done certain things that my granny didn't like, and I always had to do my chores around the house. If I *did* do something wrong, my granny would make sure that I would go to bed early and not play out. I would have to stay in the house and do extra washing up, or something like that. But my grandparents weren't strict in the sense that I couldn't speak to them. On the whole, when I hear stories about other people's grandparents, I reckon mine were pretty cool.

I was raised as a Christian and church was a must, but it was okay because they used to have the kids in one part and the adults in a different part. Then, when church was finished, there was a big field outside and all of us kids would be out there playing a game of cricket until the adults were ready to go home. They were happy times, all of us running around in the sunshine on Sunday afternoons.

When I think back to life in Jamaica, Christmas was one of my favourite times, because that was the time of the year when everybody was looking forward to the holidays. We would have time off from school, and it was the time of the year when you would probably get extra food, but also everybody would come together in one big place and all the kids would play together. Basically, you were surrounded by people. We always used to play marbles, and I was a good marble player. I would probably get a present from my parents in London, like a new shirt or a pair of trousers. We didn't have decorations. I think the decoration was more like a gathering of people instead of having a Christmas tree and stuff like that. There are enough damn trees in Jamaica anyway!

Easter is also massive in Jamaica, and we would really be looking forward to that because we knew that we would be getting extra bun and cheese, which is a spicy bun with cheese that the Jamaican people enjoy during the Easter holiday. When it came to the holidays, you would get stuff to eat that you didn't really get every day. Instead of having just a normal cup of tea, we might have a cup of hot chocolate. There would always be loads of extra food and, in a sense, everything seemed to taste sweeter.

Boxing never came up when I was in Jamaica. Back then, cricket was more like the game for us. We used to play a lot of cricket pretty much every day, because all we needed was a bat and a ball, and it wasn't hard to make your own bat, which we would make out of anything we could find when we were walking down the road.

Another thing we used to like was flying kites, and we would always make and fly our own kites. Every year, there used to be a sort of fun day at what we called the Beverly Sports Ground. It was a big open field, like a festival, and lots of people would be flying their kites. There used to be a kite competition and, believe it or not, people used to put razor blades at the end of the tail of their kites. So, if you got too close to the next kite, the razor would cut through the string and your kite would fly away, and that one would be out of the competition. The thing was, if your kite won the contest, you knew that you were going to get some money, so the competition would get pretty fierce.

In Jamaica, every day before we went to school, we had to make sure our hair was combed and our nails were nice and clean. Then you had to wait at the school gate while the teacher ran a comb through your hair. I remember one morning waking up late, and I was rushing about getting dressed for school and I didn't have time to comb my hair. So, before I left the house, I dipped my head in a basin of water. When I reached the school gate and the teacher ran the comb through my hair, a whole heap of water came flying out. It went all over the teacher and everybody else who was standing nearby, and I got caned for that because school in Jamaica was very strict.

When we would come home after school, sometimes we used to go out picking fruit, like mango and naseberry and all these things, and granny would be following behind us, watching us and telling us what to pick and where not to climb. But, as soon as she was gone, obviously we would go high in the trees and we often used to fall out of the bloody trees, but none of us ever got hurt. The great thing was that we had the freedom of going out and doing that kind of thing, which we obviously took for granted back then.

We used to eat plenty of ackee and saltfish, which is the national dish in Jamaica and is still one of my favourite meals to this day when it's cooked properly, and I am happy to say that Carmen always makes it beautifully. In fact, I have been very lucky in that respect. My granny, my mum, my wife, and now our daughters are all very good cooks. Also, my granny used to cook plenty of red pea soup and rice and peas, although, to tell the truth, I was never a big eater. Even now, I'm not a great eater, and I think that is because I have still got the boxing sort of discipline in me where you only eat so much. Also I don't want to get fat because I have been told that, if I get fat, Carmen is going, so I am still trying to show my six-pack. I'm still doing my press-ups!

1968 was the year I came over to England. I remember the day like it was yesterday when my granny said to me, 'James, your mum is coming for you and she is going to take you back to London with her.' All I knew about England was what people were telling me, that it was cold, that it was always raining or snowing, and things like that, and I couldn't bloody *believe* it when my granny was saying the words to me. I was thinking to myself, 'I'm not going to London. I don't *want* to go to London. No *way* am I going to London!' It was such a big shock to me because, up until that day, I honestly never thought that I would ever have to leave Jamaica.

All I really knew about my mum was that she used to send clothes over for me in a big trunk, and I never really got to wear any of those clothes anyway because my granny always used to tell me that I had to wait until I got bigger before I could wear them bloody clothes, and I bet those clothes are still in that damn trunk to this day! For the first nine years of my life, my granny had been the one who taught me how to wash, how to brush my teeth, how to comb my hair. My granny was the one who fed me, clothed me and guided me. My granny was the one who had corrected me, and she was the one who would bust my arse if I did something wrong.

Now that I am a parent myself, I understand the bond that forms when you raise a child, that special kind of love that you have for that child from the beginning, and there is always going to be that strong feeling between yourself and that child. That was the feeling that I had for my granny. I knew that my mum was there and that she lived very far away. But, back then, I obviously didn't understand about how people had to travel to England for a better life for their families. All I knew back then was that it was my granny who had brought me up and she was the only person I had ever known who had really looked after me. So, when I knew that my mum was coming over to get me and take me back with her, it was hard at first because that gap in time was there where I hadn't known my mum and she was like a stranger to me.

So, all of a sudden, my mum arrived and she looked just like a younger version of my bloody granny! The first time I actually met her, she says, 'I'm your mum and I have come to take you back to London with me.' I took one look at my mum and I just ran straight out of the damn house. I didn't care about this woman who was saying that she was my mum. I didn't want to leave this lovely place where I had grown up with my cousin and my Uncle Frank. I didn't want to be taken away from Carmen and her brothers and sisters. So, to be honest, I was very hostile to my mum when she first came over. I wasn't happy at all. I thought 'I'm not going with you,' and I picked up some stones and I started to throw them at her.

A funny thing happened on my last day of school before I left for England, or at least I thought it was funny anyway. We had these teachers, a man and his wife named the Teachers Arton, who were very strict. I can't remember what it was that I did now, but on my last day of school one of them caned me. So I said to the boys, 'Right, guys, we are going to stone the Teachers Arton when they come out of school in their car.' The boys followed me and they were all saying, 'Yeah,

James, we will stone their car.' So, as the Teachers Arton came driving out of school, we all pelted their car with stones. We ran off laughing and, when we got back home, my granny was cooking this big meal and the boys were all wondering why granny was cooking this big meal in the middle of the week.

So we were all sitting around the pot and we were all laughing, and the boys were all saying, 'Yeah, we stoned the Teachers Arton.' Then they said to me, 'So, James, what is going to happen when we go back to school tomorrow?' I looked at them and I just shrugged my shoulders, and I said, 'I don't know about *you* guys, but *I'm* going to London tomorrow!' It turned out that, when the boys went back to school the next morning, I got them all caned. I got them caned very hard. But I was okay because I was at the airport!

The last evening before I left for England, Carmen and me were sitting down outside the house. We had just come back from riding the donkey together one last time, and obviously I was holding her tight because I was having to say goodbye to her. She said to me, 'James, when you go to London, you must write to me.' I said, 'Of course I will write to you.' But I have to admit that, once I had settled in London, I forgot about writing to Carmen.

When me and my mum went to the airport, it was the first time I had ever seen an aeroplane that close in my life and it looked so damn big. It was huge, and there were so many people getting on this bloody plane. To me, even the *people* seemed to look big. The people just looked different to any people I had ever seen before, because I had never seen such a big crowd in my whole life. They were all different shapes and sizes and colours, and I couldn't believe that they were all going to fit inside one plane.

It was a strange experience for me and the whole thing must have tired me out, because I kind of closed my eyes and slept for most of the flight. I remember waking up when the plane was coming in to land. I was sitting next to a window, and I looked down at that moment when a plane is at a certain height, and you can see the buildings and you can see the people but it all looks so tiny. I was thinking, 'Wow! These people are small. Even *I* am bigger than these people.' Then, when the plane landed and we got into the airport terminal and I looked up at all the people around me, I was thinking, 'Damn, where have all those small people gone?'

So, at the end of the day, I left Jamaica when I was nine years old and I never went back there again until I was 47. I was pretty upset when my granny died when I was 11 years old. I honestly believed that I was going to grow up and go back to Jamaica to be with my granny, but I never saw her again. As for my mum, I would never have believed it when she came to take me away, but I *did* grow to love her very, very much. She was a brilliant mum in many ways. My mum was definitely a fighter and, no matter what problems came my way during the rest of her life, she was always in my corner.

LONDON

THE weather wasn't all that bad on the day I arrived at Gatwick Airport. I think it was probably around summertime, so it wasn't freezing cold or anything like that. The cold weather in this country would be something that I would experience later on. One of dad's friends came to collect us in a car and he drove me and my mum back to Peckham. It was one of those big Austin cars and it had one of them dogs at the back that was nodding his head. There were flowers on the dashboard and there was carpet on the floor, and I thought the car was really looking good, done out very nice. If I were to see that car now, I would be thinking, 'That car is shit! It's horrible!' But, back then, I was thinking, 'Yeah, I want one of these cars when I grow up with this little dog nodding his head at the back.'

I honestly don't know what time of day it was, but sitting in the back of that car and looking out of the window, my first impression as we drove towards London was that England seemed to be a very, very dark place. Dad's friend took us to 50 Lyndhurst Grove, which was going to be my new home.

That house is still there now and, every now and then, I go and check it out.

It was a big house and, when we lived there, it belonged to a man named Mr Lewis and he was our landlord. Mr Lewis was a black guy as well, which was shocking to me. I was thinking to myself, 'Eh? You're a black guy and you have got this big house?' Mr Lewis and his family lived downstairs. My Auntie Lovely, who had by now come over from Jamaica, was living on the middle floor, and we had two rooms right at the top, sort of a living room and a bedroom, which my mum kind of split in half with a curtain.

When people came over from the West Indies, everything they bought for their houses was flowery. The carpet was flowery. The wallpaper was flowery. The settee was flowery. They did their houses up with all this flowery stuff, bright red and yellow flowers. I think it reminded them of being at home, and that is what Lyndhurst Grove was like. There was a kitchen downstairs, which my mum and my auntie shared, and there was one bathroom. So I suppose you could say that the place was quite crowded, but it was definitely a happy home.

When I came over to England, my brother, Evans, had already been born because there is a six-year age gap between us. So, all of a sudden, there was just me and this little brother who I had never met before, and he used to be a damn nuisance! He used to be a little pest. Because I was the bigger brother, I used to do certain things and try to bully him to get the blame for it, especially when I was in the wrong. But I think mum and dad sensed certain things were happening, so I didn't manage to get away with it too often.

One time, we went out on a trip and came back a bit late, and my mum told us not to drink too much before we went to bed. That night, me and Evans crept downstairs, got inside the fridge and drank some R Whites Lemonade, which we thought was the biz at the time. I must have had too much R Whites, because I remember wetting the bed. So I changed places with my brother so that mum would think it was Evans who had wet the bed. But, when I woke up the next morning, my mum was shouting at me, 'James! You wet the bed!' I said, 'Mum, I didn't wet the bed. It was Evans who wet the bed.' But she knew I was telling stories because she said, '*He* is lying in the place where *you* went to sleep last night!'

Evans loved playing football. In fact, when Evans grew up, he actually became a semi-pro footballer and his three sons are now playing professional football. Me and Evans were playing football in the house one time and he said to me, 'Come on, you be the goalkeeper.' I didn't know nothing about football and I didn't even have a clue what a bloody goalkeeper was! So he kicked the ball towards me and I tried to kick the ball, and it went straight past Evans and it broke the damn cabinet, and I thought, 'Oh, my God, we're going to get killed.' When dad came in, he says, 'Who broke the cabinet?' So I said 'Evans.' Dad never said nothing. Dad just went upstairs. When mum come in, oh my word! She was *so* angry. Mum said, 'Who broke the cabinet?' I said 'Evans.' Mum says, 'Well, you are gonna get beat because you're the oldest.' I said, 'But *he* was the one who kicked the ball.' But mum took out the belt and mum started to beat me, saying 'I *told* you not to play football inside the house.'

Another time when me and Evans were in the kitchen messing about, we smashed some dishes. My mum was *so* upset. She says, 'You two just *wait* until your dad comes home!' That is how upset mum was. She was so upset that she couldn't even *beat* us! When my dad came home, my mum says, 'The boys were playing football inside the kitchen again.' So my dad just gave us one of his looks and he said, 'You boys be careful, and don't do it again.' Then dad went upstairs to read his *Daily Mirror*. But, in the night, we could hear 'biff, baff, biff, baff, baff', and we knew that mum was taking it out on dad because dad never did nothing to us.

I think dad got beat up for us a couple of times. Mum and dad had a couple of fights, but dad never won any of them because he wasn't that type of guy. Dad was probably the most placid dad in the world. When mum used to say, 'Wait until your dad comes home,' me and Evans used to laugh because we knew that dad wasn't going to do anything. If dad shouted at us or tried to hit us, it was only because mum wanted him to. Dad would make more noise trying to frighten you with his voice rather than anything else.

The closest dad got to beating me was when he would take the belt and he'd come upstairs, and he would be making out that he was trying to hit me, but he *knew* that he was missing me. Then Evans would go to mum and grass us up and say, 'Mum, dad is not really hitting James,' and then we would hear 'bish, bish, bash, bash', and we'd see dad the next day with bruises. So mum and dad would have their little turf war, and dad would always come out second best. He'll tell you he won the odd fight with mum, but I never saw him win one in his damn life. To make dad upset, you would really have to push the boat out. But with mum, it was just like the flick of a switch.

There were certain things that I found very surprising when I first came to England. For example, I will always remember how shocked I was when I found out that you had to actually pay for a kite. So, for a while, I was still making my own kites over here the way I used to in Jamaica, and I used to go to Blackheath to fly them. People used to look shocked when they saw me, because they were flying these big kites that they had bought in a shop and there was me with a kite that I had made myself.

It is really funny now looking back, but I couldn't believe it when I went to look inside my mum and dad's record collection and I saw that they had some bloody Jim Reeves records! I said to mum, 'But Jim Reeves is white,' and my mum said, 'It doesn't matter. This is music, and he sings good music.' I honestly couldn't believe that my black parents had white music.

I think one of the things that astonished me the most was the fact you couldn't walk in the park and just pick fruit to eat. Back in the West Indies, if you are hungry, you just go out and pick fruit, and you plant your own stuff to grow and eat. That is how you survive. When I came over to London and I realised that there was nothing to pick, I was thinking, 'How am I going to survive?' I was walking around looking for things to pick and there was nothing there. There were no banana trees to climb. I was thinking, 'What sort of country is this? I'm gonna starve! I want to go back home.'

My first school in England was Bellenden Primary School in Peckham. Our landlord's son was called Gerald and he was a year older than me, so he used to take me to school. Going to school in England for the first time was really, really strange. In a sense, it was frightening, because I expected it to be like school in Jamaica. On my first day, I remember going up the steel steps to the door and just standing there, and all the other kids were running past me and they've all gone inside. So I was still standing at the door waiting for the teacher to invite me in, because I was expecting the teacher to be checking my nails and running a comb through my hair. The teacher just looked at me and she said, 'Cook, what are you doing just standing there?' I said 'I am waiting for you to tell me to come in, Miss,' and all the kids started to laugh. But, once I started to adjust, to be quite honest, I never had so much fun in my life because, after I got used to it, there was a lot of playing going on and I was thinking, 'This is great. School is great.'

In Jamaica, compared to London, school life was very, very strict. That is why, when I came to London, I couldn't understand it. I couldn't understand the freeness in class, the freeness in school. I think, when I came over to this country, I was very, very bright. I remember being very bright in Jamaica. But, when I came to London, I think my education went downhill pretty quick because, as long as you were in school, you were good to go. In Jamaica, the teacher would be standing over you to make sure you spelt certain words correctly and you had to read certain paragraphs at the end of the day before you were allowed to go home. In London, it wasn't like that. The teacher and the class would probably read something all together and, if we couldn't read it, we would probably just skip over it. So it was a lot easier in school in London. The classroom in Jamaica would be quiet and respectful. In London, the classroom was a lot more chaotic.

I think the first time I honestly and truly understood how much love my mum had for me was when this teacher in primary school was trying to bully me, and she *really* did upset me. The next day, my mum came up the school with her brolly and she told off the teacher right in the middle of the classroom. She fixed up that teacher good and proper in front of all the other kids in the class, and that was when I realised, 'This is my mum and she's great.' Mum never stood for no nonsense. Mum would punish you if she knew you had done something wrong or you were lying about something, but she would never have any of her children being bullied or treated badly. Mum was a strong person and she would say, 'No, I'm not having that.'

When I hear the life stories of other fighters who suffered poverty and hardship when they were younger, it makes me realise how fortunate we were not to have experienced anything like that. Dad was a plasterer. I remember my dad plastering around this side of town and, sometimes after school, I used to mix the cement and the plaster for him, and he would always give me a little bit of money. Mum used to work for the Peek Freans factory, the biscuit place, which was one of the biggest companies at that time. So we never really had any hardship. If we wanted something and we didn't get it this week, we would get it a week or two weeks down the line. When the Ben Sherman shirts were coming out in loads of different colours, we used to have a new one every week. Every colour there was, we used to have, because mum used to go out to East Street Market and buy them for us.

There was one time when me and Evans asked mum for racing bikes and mum said, 'No, you're not getting no bikes.' But that was classic with mum. She might say no at first, but she would end up getting us whatever we wanted if she could. Anyway, when we came home from school one day, there were two racing bikes there, one for me and one for Evans. Then my mum sent me down to the off licence on Southampton Way in Peckham, so I rode my new bike down there and I parked it outside the shop.

When I came back outside, I was horrified to find that my brand-new bike had gone. I must have walked up and down the road for two hours looking for that damn bike. I was thinking, 'I *can't* go home without my bike. I'm gonna get *killed*!' I even saw a guy on a bike, and I chased him down the road because I thought it looked like my bike. I remember running after him, shouting, 'That's my bike. Get off! It's not your bike.' In the end, it got so late that my dad and Evans came out looking for me, and I met them up the top of the road and I said, 'Dad, somebody stole my bike.' I expected dad to go mad, but he never did. When we got home, mum was shouting at dad, saying, 'I *told* you that you shouldn't buy them no damn bikes.' But, to kill the argument, I said, 'But, mum, it was *you* who sent me to the off licence.' After that, I think she beat dad instead!

When I was about 11 years old, mum and dad moved us into a flat on the North Peckham Estate. Me and Evans shared a room and, by now, my sister, Angela, had come along, so she had her own room because she was a girl, and my mum and dad had a room downstairs.

In the following years, my mum gave birth to three more children, Simon, Brian and Lydia, and we all got along very well, as we still do today.

The North Peckham Estate was one of the biggest housing estates in London. It started from Peckham High Street and it ended at the bloody Walworth Road. It was a huge place, and a lot of people used to say that it was one of the worst estates in London, but I loved it there. There were always things to do and there were always things happening. Even though it was strange to me, I found it very exciting.

On Friday nights, mum didn't tend to do no cooking and we used to get money to go to the Kentucky Fried Chicken shop in Camberwell Green or the fish and chip shop in Peckham. So we couldn't wait for Friday nights to come around. There was this one Friday evening when my dad says, 'Go and buy some fish and chips for everybody and come straight back.' I had bought the fish and chips and I was on my way home when I met my friend, who was a guy named Johnny, and he says to me, 'James, are you coming to the funfair?' In those days, I didn't know anything about funfairs and I remember saying, 'Johnny, what is a funfair?'

Anyway, I ended up going off to the funfair with Johnny, and I was still carrying the fish and chips in my hands. When we got there, I started to play those penny machines with the change from what mum and dad had given me for our supper. Everywhere we went and everywhere I looked, there was something new, all these stalls and the bumper cars, and everything else. It was all so thrilling to me, because I had never really seen anything like a funfair before. So I didn't realise that time was getting on.

When I *did* go home about two hours later with the whole family's bloody fish and chips in my hands, I saw my dad coming down the road. The thing about my dad is he's got the worst bent leg in the world, and I saw him walking towards me with his bent leg, but dad didn't say a lot. Dad just grabbed the fish and chips from me and said, 'Where have you been?' I said, 'I went up the funfair.' The way he just looked at me, it was like, 'Mum is going to *kill* you!' I went home and, I must admit, I *did* get beat by my mum.

When we moved to the North Peckham Estate, I didn't know much about colour and how it divided people. In fact, the first girl I fell in love with in this country was when I was about ten years old, and she was a white girl with bloody ginger hair named Susan. She lived just down the road from me, and we used to walk to school together and we would come home together. But, on the estate, it was like a stand-off between black and white, and that was the first time in my life I had ever experienced that.

There used to be a big field in the middle of the flats where we used to play football, and the white kids used to play over in one part and the black kids used to play over the opposite end, so black and white didn't mix. But eventually, we all slowly started to mingle. We all joined up together, playing Knock Down Ginger and speaking to each other, and the parents started to accept that a white kid could go and knock for a black kid or a black kid could go and knock for a white kid.

There were some skinheads who lived round the flats. We knew they played football at a certain time, and we used to play when they weren't about. But, if you happened to live next door to one of them, you never had a problem. It was normally only when there was a group of them that we tended to stay out of their way. There are certain things that I remember, like when we used to go to Blackheath to fly our kites. In those days, not many black people used to go to Blackheath and we got chased a few times by the skinheads or the Teddy boys who were around at the time. They would see us and they would chase us, but they never used to catch us.

But I never really experienced racism that deep where I could say it affected me, not like it affected some people. I think my dad was probably more in the generation that suffered all the abuse more than us, but my dad didn't really speak about anything like that. Dad would just go out and do his job, and then he would come home and look after his family.

There was one time when my dad was working on this building site, and there was something there to do and he says to the guys he was working with, 'Let me have a try.' I remember him telling my mum that the way the guys looked at him was like, 'This black fella comes over here and he thinks he can do his job better than we can.' Anyway, my dad did the job, and he must have done it very well because they made him the foreman after that.

I left Bellenden School and went to Peckham Manor, which was just down the road. By now, I was really enjoying school. I liked being in class with my friends. Mind you, when school was finished at four o'clock, we would all go back across to our own estates and I must admit we were very territorial. It wasn't a matter of colour. It was just about where we lived. We would be saying stuff like, 'This is Peckham. This is *our* estate, and you can't come here from another estate and start making noise.' But, the next day, we would still all be talking to each other in school, and it was nowhere near as bad as the postcode wars that are going on nowadays.

Back then, if you got caught up in a certain area and you shouldn't be in there, there would more than likely be a fist fight. If you had a row with somebody, you would meet somewhere and you would have a fight. There would be a set of supporters over there and a set of supporters over here. Whoever won, the loser would get up, you'd both shake hands and you would call it a day. So that was the way that things got sorted out.

The only time we used to hear about a lot of fighting going on in the area was when there used to be gang fights between the football fans, the guys who supported teams like Millwall, West Ham and Leeds United. Those guys would fight in a crowd and it was always a case of throwing chairs about or they would put a bottle over someone's head, or something like that. I heard about people getting beat up, but I never heard much about anybody getting stabbed. Obviously, there *were* knives and people *did* carry knives. I mean, people *did* die fighting with knives and things like that. But, back then, if somebody died by a knife, it was much rarer than it is now.

There were four brothers on the North Peckham Estate called the Waynes and one of them got stabbed. He died in a knife fight on the estate in a place called the Pitt Street Settlement, which was a youth club, and the Wayne brothers used to run the sound system there. When I heard that one of the Waynes had got stabbed and he had died, that really shook me, because he was the first person who I ever knew who died suddenly like that. That was the first time I was hit by the reality that there are some people carrying knives out there and you can die. But, to be honest, if people were dying from being stabbed, you didn't hear a lot about it. In those days, you could walk down the road and not really worry about whether somebody had a knife.

Two of my best friends on the North Peckham Estate were Rupert Staple and Ossie Smith. We used to hang around most of the time, and we were always together. They were both a couple of years older than me and they were two completely different personalities, but they were two great guys. When mum was upset with me, Ossie would go to mum and wind it up. He would say, 'Yes, Mrs Cook, beat the boy, he is out of order.' So, therefore, mum and dad used to love Ossie, because they thought that he was the smartest one out of all of us. In actual fact, I would say that Rupert was definitely the most steady one out of the three of us in the sense that, if me and Ossie said, 'Yeah, let's go and do that,' Rupert would probably take a second to think and say, 'No, mate, we're not doing that.' Rupert was the sensible one who kept us in check.

Mind you, those guys were both very fast. I will never forget the time we were all coming back from Hackney to Peckham one night and we decided that we didn't want to walk, so we got into a cab. I was still very green, still so new to London, and I didn't know what they had in their minds. When the cab driver drove us into the estate, the boys jumped out and ran. So, all of a sudden, Rupert and Ossie were gone and I was just stuck there in the back of the cab like a blasted sitting duck. So the cab man just locked the door and drove me to Peckham Police Station. Mum wasn't very happy about that, I can tell you!

As our little gang started to grow, there was me, Rupert and Ossie, and another guy called Winston. There was a girl called Cheryl Sealey, and there was Angela, who was my first girlfriend where I seriously thought I was in love. Well, actually Angela was the second girlfriend. I have to say that a girl named Valerie was probably my first girlfriend, although I think Valerie was a couple of years older than me. To be honest, when it came to the girls, I was running around all over the shop. At that age, you want to be able to say, 'Yeah, this is my girlfriend.' Then, when Angela came on the scene, I sort of left Valerie to go with Angela. I mean, Valerie was okay. Valerie was very nice, but she got the boot because I liked Angela better.

Angela was the last one of our gang to move on to the estate, so she was very much the new girl. Angela went to Silverthorne School, which was on Southampton Way, and the rest of us went to Peckham Manor and there was Collingwood Girls' School across the road where Valerie used to go. Before Angela came along, when it came to lunchtime, us boys used to go for a walk across the road to see the girls at Collingwood Girls. But, when we discovered Silverthorne, we used to walk to Silverthorne at lunchtimes and go and speak to Angela. So, by the time we got back, we probably would be bloody late for lessons and we'd be trying to sneak in without the teachers seeing us.

There was a Turkish family called the Hussains who lived down the road, and they had four sons. One of them was named Ali and he was a good friend of mine who was also part of our gang. Ali was the one who would calm me down and stop me getting in trouble in school if I was going to react to something that somebody said or did, although Ali was quick to lose his *own* temper because he stood for no rubbish. Ali's bigger brother, Mustafa, used to be friends with one of the guys who wore skinhead boots. If I remember rightly, I think his name was Steve, and he used to walk tough like he was a hardman and we thought he was flash, so we all used to tease him and run away from him around the estate. The thing was that we honestly didn't think we were doing any harm and Steve never really chased us that much anyway, because he was friends with Mustafa and we were friends with Ali. When you think about it, life is funny, because, these days, one of Ali's sons is going out with my cousin's daughter.

I think one of the main reasons that people from outside thought that the North Peckham Estate was a frightening place was because of all the concrete walkways that connected the flats. I can still remember some of those walkways very well, like the Promenade South or the Promenade East. Once you were in there, the walkways could lead you anywhere. They kind of joined up like computer keys. We lived round there, so we got to know all the walkways, where they led to and where they didn't lead to. If we ever made any trouble and the police or anybody came in there after us, once we were back on the estate, we knew where we were going and they didn't have a clue, so we would usually get away.

I remember having a close call with this skinhead once. We walked past each other out on the street, and I think he said something to me. He had the shiny boots on with the steel toecaps and I had started to do a bit of boxing by now, so I hit him and I ran off. I have always been a good runner, but that skinhead bloody chased me all the way down Peckham High Street. I beat him on to the estate, I ran up the steps to one of the walkways and, when I got to the next level, I ducked down and hid behind a wall. Once I was out of his sight, I was lost to him, but that skinhead was walking up and down and talking to himself, and I could hear him muttering, 'If I catch that black bastard!' The funny thing was that, although I was hiding from him, I wasn't really *frightened* of him. I was just thinking, 'Damn! How the fuck did he run with them boots on and keep up with me?' That's what I was thinking about. Even then, I wasn't thinking about black and white, racism and stuff like that. I was just thinking that he was somebody who didn't like me, and it was just one of them things.

You could look out of your kitchen window at the walkway, and you could see who was coming down there. There was this one time that I will never forget when me and Angela were having an argument, and I must have shouted at her or something because Angela ran across the balcony and up the stairs to the level where she lived. At first, I ran after her, but then her mum came to the front door and I got such a fright that I just turned around and ran straight back down the balcony to our place. I was looking out of the kitchen window and that was when I saw Angela's mum marching down the walkway heading in my direction with a bad look on her face. I said, 'Mum, Angela's mum is coming!' My mum didn't say nothing, so I said, 'Mum, she's *coming*!' Then I ran upstairs to hide.

In many ways, England was back then, and still is today, a much safer place to live than Jamaica. For example, in this country, you can vote for whoever you like and it doesn't matter. But, in Jamaica, if you are walking down the road and you aren't for the right political party, they end up stabbing and killing each other, and there are only two bloody parties in Jamaica, the People's National Party and the Jamaica Labour

Party. I mean, you could go to London or anywhere in Great Britain and march down the bloody road by yourself and say that you are a new political party, and nobody will trouble you. But, over in Jamaica, it's dangerous. That is why Bob Marley was trying to bring everybody together with his music and his words.

We used to listen to a lot of reggae music, although I have to say that I didn't really appreciate Bob Marley when I was young. I liked what we called fast beat reggae, but Ossie was the one out of all of us who really loved Bob Marley. Ossie was more cultured than the rest of us, and he used to say, 'Sit down and listen to what Bob Marley is saying, and you will pick it up.' One day, we went down the record shop in Peckham to buy some music and I was going to buy something that I liked, but Ossie was saying, 'No, no, no, buy Bob Marley.' So that was the day that I bought my first Bob Marley record. It was his 'Three Little Birds' song. After that, I started to listen to Marley a lot, and I have loved him ever since.

Believe it or not, although I was having fun with my friends and enjoying going to school, it actually took a few years before I started to truly accept the fact that I wasn't going to be returning to Jamaica any time soon. I started to realise that I was still a kid and Jamaica is a long way away and, if I wanted to get back there, I would have to take a plane there on my own. I started to understand that, if I ever wanted to go back, I would have to wait until I grew up and got a job to buy an aeroplane ticket. So I started to settle down and think, 'Well, this is it. England is my home now. London is where I live.'

SPORTING LIFE

WHEN I think back to my earlier years in England, one of the things that helped me make friends easily was the fact I wasn't scared of doing stuff, particularly when it came to sport. I remember right back to when I was in primary school and they were having a sports day. The teacher was telling us to do the high jump, but nobody wanted to jump over the fence. So I went for it and I didn't exactly jump over the bar, but I kind of dived head-first over the thing. Anyway, the teacher must have liked it because she said to me, 'Can you do that again?' The teacher called the rest of the kids and the other teachers over to watch me, and I ran up to the fence and went over it head-first again. I was definitely sort of fearless when it came to sport.

To be honest, I was fighting for the ladies very early in life. The thing was, when I was growing up at school, I was a very shy guy. I was so shy, it was unbelievable. I was always at the back of the class for everything. But the funny thing was that I was never shy around the ladies. I don't know why, but that was different. That was so different. I used to have this friend in school who was named Colin Bannis. We were both in the athletics team together and me and Colin used to race each other, but Colin kept winning all the time and he was the one who was getting all the girls. So, even though we were friends, I *really* wanted to beat Colin so that *I* could get all the girls.

There was this young lady who I liked named Sonia Monteh. I was in love with Sonia, and there was her friend, Brenda Joseph, who I sort of liked as well. I liked both of them, but Sonia was the one I liked more because she was taller. We were having our last sports day before we went on to secondary school, and me and Colin were in a race out on the field. Everybody was going mad and bloody shouting out his name, and I knew that Sonia and Brenda were out there watching us, so I thought to myself, 'Colin ain't winning *nothing* today!'

As we were coming up to the home straight, Colin was beside me and I thought, 'You ain't crossing that line before me.' So I came across in front of Colin and held him up a bit so that I could run across the line first, because there was no way I was going to bloody let him beat me. The next thing I knew was all of these girls were looking at me and saying, 'You cheat! You cheat!' and that was probably the girls that I liked as well. So I started to argue with them. I was saying, 'What are you talking about? I didn't cheat. Colin never won the race. I won it!' Anyway, it turned out that, even though I finally beat Colin, I *never* got the damn girls!

Then Colin got upset with me and he wanted to fight me after school. So we started to fight. We did actually get into it, but it was stopped by a friend of ours named Trevor Miller. Trevor was the peacemaker. He was very strong. He was the strong man out of all of us. He was a muscly guy. Trevor wasn't living on the North Peckham Estate, but we used to walk home with each other a lot. My parents really loved Trevor and they showed him the same love as Trevor's parents showed me, so it was all good. Mind you, I have to say that Trevor was shit at running!

The game that I really loved was cricket. I was on the school cricket team from the time that I started to go to primary school, and also me, Rupert and Ossie used to play cricket all the time on the estate. The two of them were bloody good at cricket, and I was probably the quickest one to get out because I wasn't a great batsman, so I would be bowling all day because they were good at bowling *and* batting. In fact, Rupert and Ossie both ended up going around the world playing cricket. But, back in those days, we all played for a team in Peckham named Sabina, which I ended up staying with right up until I was in my twenties, and the Sabina team is still going now. The reason I liked the name Sabina was because it reminded me of Jamaica, because Jamaica has got a cricket pitch in Kingston called Sabina Park.

Before I got into boxing and started taking it seriously, if there was one sport that I was going to play and get picked for, it was rugby, because I used to be so quick. I played for the Peckham Manor team and, when I got hold of that ball and I started to run, I used to go left, go right, stop, turn, and I used to do all of that sort of footwork. If someone thought they were faster than me, I used to like to run them down. I liked to tackle them or show them a pass, or something like that, to show them that I was the better man. But the only problem for me as far as rugby was concerned was the footwear. Rugby players wear special rugby boots, but I never used to wear them because I was no good when I did. So I was great at playing rugby as long as I could wear my trainers.

I always fancied myself as an excellent runner. Back in Jamaica, I always wanted to run faster than Carmen's brothers. I always wanted to be running faster than my Uncle Frank. I even used to race the bloody dog in Jamaica. We had a black dog named Pearl. She was good as gold, and you'd say to Pearl, 'Go!' and then we would be racing the damn dog. So, when I came to this country, I always used to think, 'I come from Jamaica. I love running. You can't beat me.' I used to love to race my friends round the schoolyard and I always used to beat them.

The first time I ever went to Crystal Palace running track, I thought I was going to be the fastest runner there, but I ended up coming last in the 400-metre race and I wasn't happy about it. I was looking at these other kids and I was thinking to myself, 'How the hell did they beat me round this track?' So then I went up against them again in the 800-metre race and I thought I would get a bit of pride back, but I still only came third. The problem was the damn shoes again. I was fine in my trainers, but putting on a pair of running shoes and going round the track wasn't so easy. When the guys who I used to beat in the school playground were on the spikes, they used to beat me.

SPORTING LIFE

On the estate, we were playing football a lot and a little bit of skill actually started to come into my game, so I started playing a bit of football in school. Some of those boys in school used to be bloody good. But the thing with me was that, if you kicked the ball, I would run after it, I'd bloody beat you to get it, but I never had the skills when I *had* the damn ball. It was them blasted shoes again! When I put on my trainers, I wasn't too bad. I could sort of control the ball. But, when I put on a pair of football boots, that was it. I was rubbish.

From my earliest memories in Jamaica, I have always loved one-on-one competition. I have always wanted to come out on top. I have always wanted to be a winner. I have always wanted to be the best. So, in the end, boxing was the sport that I decided to make my own, and thankfully I never had no problems with boxing boots.

BOXING BEGINNINGS

I HAVE always loved Muhammad Ali from when I was a young boy. I used to be in the playground saying to the other boys, 'Okay, you be Joe Frazier and I will be Muhammad Ali.' I would hit my friends and start dancing about and, in my mind, I was floating like a butterfly and stinging like a bee. So I suppose that it all started from there really.

It was Rupert who took me down my first boxing gym. He took me down the Lynn Boxing Club. I got in the ring with this little white kid and, no matter how hard I tried, I just couldn't hit him. I am going to be honest and say that he kicked the shit out of me in there. So I picked up my stuff to leave and I said, 'I'm not staying here now, but I am coming back for you.' A little while later, Rupert told me, 'There's a boxing club in Camberwell Green and they are closing it down because they haven't got nobody going down there.' We were spending all our time just running around the estate and we never had nothing much going on at the time, so a few of us went down there to have a look.

The club was named East Lane Boxing Club, and the trainers there were named Jimmy Redwell and Ronnie White.

The first night I walked into East Lane, I started to train, and Jimmy had a look at me and he says to me, 'You're not bad.' After that, a whole heap of us started to go there and train regular three nights a week and all of a sudden the club was busy again, so they decided to keep it open. Rupert used to box as an amateur. He used to be a heavyweight. Ossie did try the boxing, but boxing wasn't for him because Ossie was a pretty boy. Ossie was a ladies' man, and he was a very good reader and writer. When it came to education, Ossie was sharp. So he trained at the boxing, but it was just to keep himself fit.

My relationship with Jimmy Redwell and Ronnie White was brilliant. They were like a pair of fathers to me. They used to take me out for something to eat. They used to take me inside their homes. They would treat me as their own and their families treated me as their own. So I must have grown up lucky because I grew up with these two great white guys looking after me. Sometimes, Jimmy and Ronnie used to stop off round my mum and dad's place, and my parents used to give them white rum. They would go there sober and then they would leave a bit wobbly, and their wives used to say, 'Don't let them have none of that damn rum no more.'

Another great bloke at the gym was a fella named Ray Hole. Ray was the club secretary and he also did the matchmaking. Ray wasn't that much older than us and it was so funny, because he was the only blond-haired kid amongst all of us black kids in the club. Ray would get in the ring with me, and I used to just hold him and let him punch me in my stomach. Sometimes, if I had a fight coming up, I used to have

Ray doing that for four or five rounds, and it was great for strengthening the body.

Ray was very good at drawing. He used to come in the gym with a pen and paper and, while we were standing around chatting or whatever, he would be sketching one of us. He used to catch people with his drawings really quick. But, at the time, we couldn't understand what a great talent he had. We used to just think he was bloody mad! Ray would draw you looking like a cartoon character or something, but we didn't appreciate it back then. It is only as you get older that you get to appreciate and understand real talent, and what it means when people have got real talent.

I had my first amateur bout when I was 14. I can't remember it all that clearly, but I think I won it. Up until that first fight, I had just been messing about in the gym if I am really going to be honest. I had no understanding of controlling myself in those days. Whereas Jimmy and Ronnie were teaching us to box with our hands up, all I had to do was see a person's face and I would just run straight at them throwing quick, hard shots. But, in time, thanks to Jimmy and Ronnie's patience and knowledge and the help that Ray Hole gave me, I began to settle down. The things that they were teaching me were starting to make sense.

There used to be a lot of boxing clubs around in them days and amateur matches were so much easier to make back then than they are today. Mind you, there was one type of fight that I never wanted to have. The thing was a lot of the guys at school used to box, so you may have three or four boys in your class at the same weight and fighting for different clubs. So, if you were in the same weight as somebody else who was in your class, you could end up boxing them and I never wanted to do that. What you didn't want to do was lose to somebody in your class from a different club. There would have been chaos, so I always avoided that. But I remember two guys called Eric and Dennis that never avoided that and, when Eric beat Dennis, Dennis got teased every day, and there was no way that I was having that. They crucified each other because one beat the other one. Funnily enough, I saw Dennis a couple of months ago at my dad's 82nd birthday party.

The atmosphere in the East Lane gym was brilliant, and there was nothing about colour, race and all this stuff. Our trainers and our matchmaker were white guys and we were mostly black guys, and everybody just came in and worked hard, and we would all have a laugh together. Then we would finish and we'd go home, and that would be it. On the way to the gym and back, I used to travel between Peckham and Camberwell Green with my kit, and I used to tie my boxing gloves on my bag to show people that I was boxing. I think I used to do that partly because I was proud of being a boxer, but also I think it was so that people would see the gloves and know that I was boxing, so nobody would say anything bad to me and I never had any problems with anybody.

Mind you, once you went outside of London, sometimes it was a different story. Ronnie White originally came from Devon, and he took me down there one time and he told me to go inside a shop for something or other. When I went inside that shop, I will never forget it. It was like everybody froze. It was like, 'Hey, you're black. What are you doing in this shop?' So then Ronnie came in. Ronnie was a policeman, and he said, 'It's all right, he's my boy.' After that, everybody relaxed a little bit.

I think I was about 16 when I started to feel that I wanted to take boxing seriously, and it was also at that time I realised what a hard sport boxing could be, in more ways than one. Ronnie and Jimmy took me to Brighton to box this guy, and I think his name was Dave Cole. He had boxed for London and England, and he was a white guy. He had all the badges sewn on his shorts, and he was so flash. The first round, he boxed my head off. The second round, I came back to the corner and I said to Jimmy, 'I thought you said white men can't dance!' I mean, this guy was dancing all *over* me. So Ronnie looked at me and said, 'Right, go out there and knock him out now,' which I did.

When I went to collect my trophy off this old lady, she was really clinging on to that damn trophy as if she didn't want to give it to me. So I had to sort of pull the blasted trophy away from her. I said to her, 'Give it to me. I won it. It's mine.' That was when I realised that they hadn't wanted me to win and, what is more, they hadn't been *expecting* me to win, which shocked me quite a lot because I never thought you would get that sort of thing happening in the amateurs. But, when we were driving back to London that night, it was an amazing feeling for me, because I had just upset a popular guy in his own town who they never expected me to beat, and I had my damn trophy too!

I think I upset the script quite a few times as an amateur. I remember beating a guy named Tony Godfrey from Repton Boxing Club. Repton was known as the top club in London, and their boxers were winning everything back then. We were boxing at York Hall and I think it was an ABA championship fight, and this was the first time I'd ever had any experience with Tony Burns, the trainer at Repton who was well-known for swearing a lot. When the bout was finished, Tony looked at me and he says, 'Fucking hell, Cook, you done it again!' I was so surprised that my mouth was hanging open, and I said to Ronnie, 'He just *swore* at me!' Ronnie just looked at me and he said, 'Don't worry, James, that's just Tony. He does that all the time.'

My mum always supported me in my boxing, but the thing with mum was that she would get overexcited because she always wanted to defend me. I was boxing at Manor Place Baths one time, and my mum and my auntie came along to support me. The guy I was boxing was massive. He was full of muscle, and he was absolutely huge. So, when mum saw the guy coming out to box, she got up with her brolly and she started coming towards the ring. I turned around and saw her and I said, 'Mum, what are you *doing?*' Then my auntie told her to sit down. That was the last time I ever brought my mum to a boxing show, because she was that protective over me and she liked to get up and fight.

I became sort of the biggest name inside the East Lane gym, so everybody who came in wanted to spar with me and, because of that, I learnt a lot about discipline. When I sparred with the ones that were good, obviously I had to be running around to keep out of the way. But, with the ones that were not so good, I knew better than to take liberties. Whenever I was matched up to box, there was always plenty of sparring.

With Ronnie being a policeman and Jimmy being an electrician for the *Daily Mirror*, sometimes they both had to work a bit late, and Jimmy used to phone me up and ask me to take the training session. So I used to go down the club and I used to tell them, 'Right, guys, Jim and Ron can't come tonight, so I will be taking the class.' There was an older guy than me in the gym called Shefton and Jimmy never really asked Shefton to help out. He only asked me. So, when I would say that I was taking the class, Shefton sometimes used to get a bit upset and, when I used to spar with him, he used to try and bash me up.

I had no way of knowing it at the time, but this was to be the start of my life in youth work. I noticed over time that, when I was taking the class, they might come in there looking a bit miserable, but there would always be a smile on their faces when we finished, and that was when I found out that I could teach a class, that I had the ability to get everybody smiling and happy, and I just carried on like that. I think it was from there on that I said to myself, 'Whatever happens, this is what I want to do,' in the sense that I wanted to work with young people.

By the time I was 17, my mum and dad had moved to Dulwich and me and Angela had moved into a flat together on the North Peckham Estate. There was a youth club in Dulwich that was just across the road from where my mum and dad lived. Because of the experience I was getting with Ronnie and Jimmy, I started off at the youth club as a volunteer with no pay, just helping out, doing fitness and racing with the kids. They would challenge me to do press-ups or sit-ups, and I would teach them to shadowbox. In the end, the council who were running the club decided to pay me and I ended up staying there for about five years.

In Peckham, Jim was also training a football team and, when he couldn't get there, I used to take the football class for him. Don't ask me how, but I ended up sort of managing that football team. The funniest thing was I still didn't have a damn clue about football! The only thing I knew about football was that Pelé was the greatest footballer in the world.

In the end, I had 26 fights in the amateurs and I won 20 of them. To be quite honest, one of the reasons I suppose I didn't have a lot of fights as an amateur was because most of my wins were stoppages and, when that happens, it becomes much harder to find somebody to box. Also, I broke my hand a couple of times as an amateur, which was something that would cause me problems throughout my entire boxing career.

I can remember clearly the first time it happened. I was queuing up to see the doctor at a boxing show at York Hall and this bloke was standing behind me. He was smaller than me, but he was the same weight as me, and he says, 'Who are you boxing?' I looked down at him and I said, 'I don't know. Who are *you* boxing?' He says, 'I am boxing Jimmy Cook and, if he thinks he's gonna knock me out tonight, he's got a different story coming.' Anyway, the fella went into the ring first and, when he saw me coming, it was like he was frozen! As soon as the bell went, I went out and I hit him with my right hand, and that was the first time I broke my hand.

I had some tough fights in the amateurs, and I didn't always agree with the decision if it went against me. When I fought Conrad Oscar as an amateur, I thought I won the fight. Conrad was a hardcase who came originally from the Dominican Republic. He had made his home in Paddington, so we were two Londoners up against each other. I always liked a good punch-up. But, if I thought that my opponent was too tough, I would divert to the second plan and use my boxing skill to outsmart them. I knew that Conrad Oscar was extremely tough, but boxing-wise I don't think he beat me. Anyway, he got the decision against me, but I didn't believe that he got the better of me. Then, the week after my fight with him, it said in *Boxing News*, 'After beating Cook, Oscar goes pro.' I remember I was really upset when I saw that because I wanted to box Conrad Oscar again and get my revenge. I *did* box him again after I turned professional, but I will get to that later.

Things are not always how you first think they might be when it comes to boxing. I boxed for the London squad against Budapest at one of the big hotels in London. I think it could have been the Royal Lancaster. We were all lined up in the ring with the two teams facing each other, and we were all facing our opponents. I saw a big guy standing in front of me at first, but then they shuffled along and I was suddenly looking at a different bloke who was very little. But I still thought that I was going to be boxing the big bloke and I was thinking to myself, 'Damn! He's big.' But then, when the fight came, it turned out that my bloke was the little one. He wasn't the man that I had got my mind set on, and I was thinking, 'Where has the big guy gone?' It turned out that the little guy had the best record out of all of them. He was the Budapest champion and I won against him, but I must admit that he *did* give me a tough fight.

I reached two London ABA finals, both against a fighter named Johnny Graham, and both took place at the Royal Albert Hall. I used to hear about this great venue and I used to think that the Albert Hall was just a place for rich people to go. To me, I was just a boy off the street doing my stuff, and I used to believe that a black man from Peckham probably couldn't even pay to go and see a performance at the Albert Hall, so to actually go there and box was just fantastic. It was out of this world even to see the venue itself, never mind box there. In my head, because it was the Royal Albert Hall, it felt like one of the royal family was there somewhere watching me.

When I boxed Johnny Graham the first time, I didn't think that he beat me. But he had the two biggest promoters and managers in Britain looking at him, which was Mickey Duff and Terry Lawless, and also Johnny had a much better record than me. He was one of the big-name fighters around at the time who they reckoned was going to be a bright prospect.

You see, East Lane was a very small club, so nobody did the East Lane boxers any favours. If we found ourselves up against any of the lads from the big clubs such as Eltham or Repton, we *really* had to win good to get a result and, when I say 'win good', it would probably have to be a stoppage. If a fight went the distance against some of these big clubs, we would often struggle to get the decision. In a fair world, even if you are boxing against the favourite, if you beat him you should get the result. This is when you realise that boxing can be so unfair.

The second time I boxed Johnny Graham in the ABA finals, I thought to myself, 'Okay, I got robbed in the first one. Am I going to get robbed again in the second one? No bloody way!' So I trained like a devil for the rematch. I was running up and down the hill in Dulwich. I was outside my mum's front door in Dulwich shadowboxing. People used to stare at me as if they were thinking, 'What is this guy doing?' I used to run around Peckham backwards, trying to do all the Ali stuff. I was speaking to myself like Muhammad Ali. I was twisting and turning. I was sprinting from lamp post to lamp post and shadowboxing. Ali was in my head, no matter what I did. He was my hero, so I wanted to be like him. I was thinking to myself that no way was Johnny Graham going to beat me this time.

In the end, my second fight with Johnny Graham went the same way as our first. In fact, I thought I won the second one even more clearly than I won the first one, but the judges gave him the decision over me again. I was very upset, and I will always remember what Jimmy Redwell said to me afterwards. Jimmy said, 'James, if you are going to get robbed, you might as well get robbed *and* get paid for it.'

Looking back now at my professional career, I can see clearly what Jimmy Redwell meant when he was saying those words to me. Jimmy understood what the boxing game was all about, and that was his way of telling me that I would be better off getting a pro licence and earning some money, even if I wasn't always going to be in the winning corner. But, at the time, I was so pissed off with that second bad decision against Johnny Graham that I didn't really ask Jimmy what he meant because, in all honesty, at that moment I didn't *care* enough to ask. I was just feeling very angry and very down, and all I could think about was the unfairness of it all. After that fight, I never boxed as an amateur again.

CARMEN

ONE day in 1976, I had the surprise of my life when my Auntie Lovely told me that my childhood sweetheart, Carmen, had left Jamaica and had come over to live in London. My auntie was having a party at her house in Bermondsey and she said, 'James, you should come to the party and see Carmen.' Anyway, I took myself along to my auntie's party and I was so confident, or maybe it was something else other than confidence, but I took Angela along with me too! When I arrived at Auntie Lovely's place, Carmen was already there with her parents and, from the first moment I saw her again after all those years, I thought to myself, 'Damn! I wish I *had* written to her now!' She was slim, she had a good figure, and she really looked great. Mind you, I'm not saying that my girlfriend, Angela, didn't look good. She *did* look good because, trust me, I was a very fussy guy!

I don't know if Carmen was a little bit pissed off with me when she first saw me because I hadn't written to her, but I reckon the truth is that she probably loved me so damn much that her heart must have melted as soon as she saw me. As for me, if I am honest, seeing Carmen again must have really thrown me because that was the first time that I remember ever getting drunk, so much so that I had to go and have a little lie down.

Anyway, there I was, pissed out of my head, lying on a bed round my auntie's place, and suddenly the door to the bedroom opened and I had Angela sitting one side of me and Carmen sitting on the other side. They had both made me coffee, and I remember Angela saying to me, 'James, do you want a cup of coffee?' I said, 'No.' So Carmen said to me, 'James, do you want a cup of coffee?' and I said, 'Yes'.

That was the beginning of the end for Angela and me. For the next six months, I was back and forth between Peckham and Hackney because I wanted to see Carmen. I had just bought my first car, which I named Samantha. I think I used to read about Samantha Fox, and the name Samantha just grabbed me. I was working in a sheet metal place at the time and we used to have nice bright blue paint at work for the filing cabinets that we used to make, so I sprayed Samantha with this beautiful blue colour and that car was my pride and joy.

One night, I went over to see Carmen at her parents' house in Hackney and I parked Samantha outside in the street. I pretended to leave at a certain time and, after Carmen's mum and dad had gone to bed, I sneaked back into the house. So me and Carmen were downstairs in the living room and we ended up falling asleep. Then, all of a sudden, we woke up pretty sharpish when we heard a key in the front door.

Carmen's dad must have gone out early for his newspaper or something, and he was letting himself back into the house.

Man! I was so frightened that I got up and I jumped straight through the blasted window! I got into the car very quick, but the damn thing wouldn't bloody start. So I pushed the car down the road and I left it on the corner. Then I ran all the way home, and I honestly thought that Carmen's dad didn't know anything about it. But, a couple of weeks down the line, Carmen's dad said to me, 'James, do you *really* think I didn't see that car outside the house?' That car was so damn bright that you couldn't *miss* it.

Every Friday night, Carmen's dad used to drink whiskey. So, on a Friday, I used to buy him a bottle of whiskey to soften him up. I also used to buy sweets for Carmen's younger brother and sister, David and Sharon. It was like a bribe to get them out of the way so that Carmen and I could be on our own. Every Friday night, Sharon used to come running along the balcony and she would jump all over me. She used to say, 'James, where are my sweets?' So I would give her the sweets to get rid of her. It was funny because I looked at Sharon the other day and I said, 'Fuck! I'm glad that you don't run and jump on me no more because you're too heavy now,' which made her laugh because Sharon has got a good sense of humour.

In the end, Angela gave me an ultimatum. She said to me, 'You have to make a choice.' Angela was a great girl, but I knew by then that Carmen was the one I wanted to be with. So my relationship with Angela came to an end and I moved over to Hackney to be with Carmen. We moved into a one-bedroom flat, which is just across the road from this house where we still live today.

CARMEN

The honest truth is that, I don't know about Carmen, but I was deeply in love from the first moment I saw her again. But, because we had been away from each other for so many years, once we moved in together properly, we had to find out certain things about each other. We began to discover what was acceptable and what was not acceptable for both of us. Obviously, I had been living in London for a number of years by this time, but Carmen was still new to this country, so there were differences between us in that regard. But we were in love, and we have built up a very strong bond that we have continued to share for over 40 years.

Carmen turned out to be an excellent homemaker, and she did everything for me right from the start, which she still does today. Carmen is a very good cook, which has been very lucky for me because I have never bloody cooked in my life. What is more, we hadn't been together all that long before we had another mouth to feed living under our roof.

Because I was the big brother of my family, when I moved away to Hackney and left the rest of the family over the other side of town in Dulwich, I used to keep an eye on my brothers and sisters. Angela and Simon were very good. Angela was never no trouble, and I have to say that Simon was good as gold. In fact, we used to call Simon a jacket, which is a Jamaican slang word for not our biological brother. We used to call him that because he is so clever that he speaks three different bloody languages. I had to punch Brian a few times to keep him in check, but he was fine after that. I would say that it was Lydia who was the most lively out of them all. By the time she was about 14 years old, my mum was starting to experience some difficulties with her mental health. The family were worried that mum was on the verge of a nervous breakdown, and we felt that it would be better if Lydia came to stay with me and Carmen for a while. So I went over to Dulwich to pick her up and Lydia ended up staying with me and Carmen until she was around 17. I have to say that Carmen took all of that in her stride very well and she was brilliant.

Carmen used to come and support me when I was boxing as much as she could, and her parents did as well. I think I gave one of the biggest trophies I ever won from boxing to Carmen's mum, and her parents became like a second mum and dad to me. I used to spend a lot of time round at Carmen's mum and dad's place, and they were great because they loved me. Whenever me and Carmen used to argue and she'd tell her parents about it, they would tell *her* off! Carmen's mum was great. She would say, 'What are you upsetting James for? Don't upset him. Has he had something to eat? Have you done something to him? You know he has got to train.'

During our lives together, Carmen and I have been blessed with four wonderful daughters, and all of our girls are completely and utterly different in their ways. Our first was born on 28 March 1982. We named her Lisa and I gave her the middle name of Samantha after that damn car of mine that I loved so much.

My mum had me when she was 16 years old. But, when I was a teenager, I would never have been man enough to be a father. I knew that you have got to be responsible to have a child, to bring someone into this world, and that frightened me. But, by the time I was in my early twenties, I would see some of my friends out and about and they would tell me that they were married with kids, and it was starting to run through my mind that I had reached the age when I was ready to become a dad. In my head somewhere, I was definitely thinking, 'When am *I* going to have a child?'

So having my first child was great because I was thinking, 'I am a man now.' I'd be pushing the pram down the road and people would say, 'Whose child is that?' I'd say, 'She's mine. This is my daughter.' That used to make me feel so proud. But I was also aware that I had responsibilities now and my life was never going to be the same again. I knew that my new daughter was relying on me and I had to start taking life a bit more serious now instead of playing around so much.

Lisa will always be my first baby and, when the other three decide they want to go against me, then I know that Lisa will always back me. She is a manager in the council now and she definitely takes after her dad, in the sense that she is a very hard worker and she doesn't like to see questions being unanswered, and she likes to see things getting done. Where Lisa definitely *doesn't* take after her dad is in the sense that she speaks with very clever words!

Our next baby girl came along on 13 December 1984, and we named her Keisha. I suppose you could say that Keisha was an early Christmas present, and it was nice to be a man and have my own family, especially at Christmas time. We used to have our own little private Christmas at our place, and then the rest of the family would all get together around Carmen's mum and dad's place or my mum and dad's place. We would all arrive at a certain time, and everybody would be cooking and bringing food along. So it was like one big family and everything was beautiful.

I think, if I had ever had a son who was going to box, it would have been Keisha and, what is more, she would have been a champion because she would control the whole family when she was small. Even today, where the rest of the girls might just be chilled, Keisha is the first one to put her fists up. She is like the protector of her sisters and, if they are out and something happens, Keisha will be the first one to react and the girl ain't scared to tell you if she thinks you are in the wrong. In many ways, I can see a lot of my mum's temperament in Keisha. In fact, my mum always used to look at Keisha and she would say, 'You are the one who favours me. You are the one who looks like me.'

Carmen gave birth to our third daughter on 27 March 1987, and we named her Jamie. There is a calmness in Jamie that I think she gets from me and Carmen. Jamie is very easy-going, and you really have to push her for her to get mad. I call Jamie Miss Posh, because she likes to walk down the road looking glamorous with her long, painted nails and her pretty this and pretty that. Jamie is the one who will really watch what she's eating because she wants to stay slim. The other girls are all lovely-looking young ladies who take care of themselves, but the others don't focus on that stuff in quite as much detail as Jamie does.

As our daughters began to grow up, it was great to be in a position where I could give my own kids advice in the same way as my parents and my Auntie Lovely and Carmen's parents had given me advice over the years. In those days, obviously I was still pretty young and I wanted to challenge anybody who did something that I didn't like, so I had grown used to that part of my make-up. I knew very well that it was there. But I have to say that I was shocked at just how much fatherhood definitely brought out the protective side of my nature. I was so damn protective over my girls, it was unreal. If they went to school and they came home with a tiny little scratch, I would be their big boxer dad going straight up the school and demanding to know, 'Why has she got this scratch?'

I have always said to my girls, 'Listen, I've got my eyes on you lot. There is nowhere in England that you lot can go and I won't find out what you are doing, so there is no escape.' One day, when Keisha was about 19 years old, she was walking up the road, talking to somebody on her phone, and she was swearing. I was in America at the time and, when I came back, I said to Keisha, 'Who were you swearing at on the phone?' Keisha says to me, 'Dad, you weren't even in the country!' I said, 'It don't matter that I wasn't in the country because somebody phoned me up and told me they saw you walking up the road swearing!'

One day, Jamie was walking down the road and she sees this boy looking at her and, with her being a young woman, I think she must have rather liked this boy because she was quite happy about it. So the boy came over to talk to Jamie and he asked her, 'What is your name?' She said, 'My name is Jamie Cook.' So the boy says to her, 'Are you James Cook's daughter?' Jamie said, 'Yes.' So the boy said, 'Okay, bye!' and he was straight off up the road. Jamie was so upset when she got home. She thought that I was cramping her style. I said to her, 'You see, I am even looking out for you when I'm not there.'

Carmen took to motherhood so naturally. What with her granny being a midwife, Carmen grew up with a lot of instinct about what it is to be a mum. People tend to have big families back in Jamaica and Carmen's sisters were all having kids, so Carmen has always been very knowledgeable when it comes to what to do for a child and what to give a child. If somebody in our house was not well, the first thing I would say was, 'Go to the chemist,' because I was talking like an Englishman. But Carmen would say, 'No, we can use this or do that,' and she would find things that we already had in the house. So, whenever the kids would come to me and tell me that something was wrong with them, I would say, 'Don't ask me. Ask your mum.' Carmen really is good at that side of things.

My mum, my Auntie Lovely and Carmen's mum were all very strong women who would do anything on earth for their kids, and Carmen grew up the same. To a certain extent, Carmen is pretty old-school in her ways, in the sense that she spent a lot longer than me in Jamaica and she thinks the West Indies rules are the best. To Carmen, the rules over here were not strong enough and, when the girls were born, she would want to follow the Jamaican way of raising them.

So there would be me shouting and saying, 'No, that don't work over here,' and Carmen would be saying, 'This works in Jamaica. This is how you treat them. This is what you do. This is the way that we were treated, and we all came out well and good.'

The final addition to our family arrived in our home not long after I retired from boxing. Carmen's sister, who lived in Jamaica, sadly passed away, and her daughter, who is named Patricia Harris, came over to London to live with us. Patricia had a brother named Peter and he came over to England later. But, because I had the girls, I always felt that, with girls, you have got to look after them. You've got to look after a girlchild in a slightly different way. When we heard the sad news about Carmen's sister, I asked, 'Who is Patricia going to be staying with now?' Carmen told me that the girl was going to be staying with her stepdad over in Jamaica. So we decided that Patricia should come over here and live with us because we already had everything here for our girls. We decided that living with us was the best place for her to be.

Patricia was 14 years old when she first came over and she was a sort of shy little schoolgirl, but she fitted into our family very well and she is every bit my daughter now. Patricia is great. Patricia don't like fuss, but, if she has to stand up for her own, then she will come through. These days, she is doing accounting for Hackney Council and I tease her every day because I say, 'Your council is taking too much bloody rates off me!' But Patricia has always been really good at numbers, so that is a great job for her.

Carmen has always been totally supportive of everything that I have ever done. When I was boxing, there were times when Carmen used to wake up and come out running with me. If I was thinking that I couldn't face getting up out of bed on any particular day for one reason or another, Carmen would wake up early, at four or five o'clock in the morning, and she would force me to get up and get ready to go out. Then we would drive over to Hackney Marsh and we would start running, and you can tell that Carmen is from Jamaica because she used to run like Usain Bolt!

I will never forget one morning when me and Carmen were out running towards the end of my professional boxing career. The man who was my trainer had started training the Commonwealth and European heavyweight champion at the time, Henry Akinwande. When me and Carmen got to the marshes, the pair of them were also over there to do their running. So I said to Carmen, 'If Henry Akinwande catches you up and passes you, you ain't coming back home. I'm locking the door!' So Carmen ran her little heart out, God bless her. She really *did* bloody run. These days, Lisa goes to the gym every morning. So I asked her one day, 'Why don't you pay *me* the money and I will make you lose some weight?' So Lisa says, 'No, dad, because mum still tells us about the time when you took her out running and you nearly killed her!'

The thing is, I am a man and we all know that men are always right! Particularly when I was younger, there would be times when me and Carmen would sit down and discuss things. She might say something that I didn't want to hear, and I couldn't help myself. I would be thinking that I am the man and Carmen doesn't know better than I do. But, now that I am an old man looking back at our lives together, trust me, whatever Carmen says has been right at least 99 per cent of the time, but I don't let her know that!

During the years, as our family has grown and my careers in boxing and youth work have taken up so much of my time, Carmen has been the solid one. She has always been the one who is there to look after the family and take care of the household. On top of that, Carmen is a brilliant hairdresser and, while I have been given the freedom to go off and do what I wanted to do, Carmen was out working in a hairdressing shop to help keep everything going financially, which is why I have had the freedom in the first place. Without a woman as fine as Carmen by my side, I honestly don't think I would have achieved half of what I have achieved.

After I retired from boxing, we decided that the time was right to buy a property. We were lucky because an old school friend of mine named Ernest Gill was involved in property and, when I told him that I didn't want to buy in the area where I lived because it was ex-council, Ernest laughed and he said, 'James, if you really think that, you are stupid because it's the best deal you are ever going to get in your life.' That turned out to be great advice and the house is ours now. But, back in the earlier years, there were times that we might have lost our home if it hadn't been for Carmen keeping everything going with her hairdressing. If Carmen came to me tomorrow and she said to me, 'James, I want this house and I need you to go,' in all honesty, I know that she would probably deserve the house.

Me and Carmen were rolling along quite happily as the years went by and we finally got married in 2006, which came as a bit of a surprise to me at the time, but that is something that I will say more about when it comes to that part of my story in this book. But let me just say this. As a life partner, Carmen has been wonderful.

There is hardly anybody like Carmen out there, and her sister is the same. They grew up in a generation that was dictated by the mentality back home in Jamaica, where everything is stricter, but they have got such great hearts. They can cook. They can clean. Their kids never go dirty. They will work around the clock to make sure that their house and their kids are well cared for and properly looked after. I have probably been the one who was always joking around, and Carmen is the one who has really held it all together. If I am honest, I probably haven't always been the easiest man in the world to live with and Carmen has put up with a lot. I reckon that I have been truly blessed because God gave me such a wonderful wife, and I couldn't ask for no better.

THE GRAFTER

MY DAD always wanted to teach me plastering. I think that he had it in his mind that he wanted me to go to work with him when I left school. But the thing was that it was never on my agenda to go and work with dad. I went with him one time when they were plastering this house that never had no damn windows. It was freezing cold in there and I thought to myself, 'I don't want this.' I knew that if I worked with my dad, I would have become a qualified plasterer or something like that, but I didn't want it. The thing was I wanted to be my own man.

I still had the idea in my head that I had picked up from my Uncle Frank in Jamaica about becoming a motor mechanic, so I signed up at Wandsworth College to learn how to be a mechanic. But, that winter, it was so damn cold. So I used to leave the house every morning, but instead of going to Wandsworth I used to divert to Bermondsey, where my auntie lived, and I stayed up there for about six months in the warmth without going to college. When the weather started to get a bit better, I went back up the college and I said to the bloke,

'Right, I am ready to start now. Where is my class?' He looked at me a bit funny and he said, 'They've done their qualification and they have gone. The class is finished now.' So that was the end of that.

After I realised that the motor mechanic thing wasn't going to work out, I got a job in a sheet metal place. The company used to make filing cabinets and it wasn't hard work. It was just cutting metal, and I loved putting on an overall and going into a workplace and actually earning money. After a little while, they sent me upstairs to help the guy who made the cabinets. So, from downstairs, I went upstairs to the second floor and I was making the cabinets now with the guys, putting in the drawers, using what you call a spot-welding machine and putting the cabinets together. We were earning 50p an hour and, when I tell the kids that now, they laugh. My wages after tax were about £16-something, and we used to work from eight o'clock in the morning until five o'clock at night.

In the meantime, I was still helping Jimmy Redwell out with the football team in Peckham, but the team were going to split up. There were a good bunch of guys at work and we used to enjoy a kickabout in our lunch hour, so I spoke to some of them and we decided that we would make a team. I roped in a few of the guys I knew who were boxing and who could play football, and we were good to go. But, first of all, we needed some money to register the team with the football league. There was a Peckham boy who wanted to play for us called Raymond Thomas, who used to have a sound system, so Raymond held a dance at one of the guy's houses so that we could collect enough money and go and register the team, which we did the following Monday.

Raymond Thomas was actually our goalkeeper, and his nickname used to be 'Puss' because he could be very sharp and quick. But the funny thing about Raymond was that, when he was drunk, he was a fantastic keeper and nothing got past him. So, if I saw Raymond coming and he was staggering a little bit, he was going straight in goal. He was that bloody good when he'd had a little drink. He'd be diving all over the place and he would catch everything. But, when Raymond was walking straight, we knew it was going to be a shit day because we knew that he was going to let in everything and we were going to get beat. In the end, Raymond left and went and played for a couple of teams. He eventually became a fireman in Peckham and he goes around teaching fire safety now.

On Saturday and Sunday mornings, we used to get the team out playing. I never used to teach them football, but I used to do the keep fit side of it. There was another guy in work who was helping me out and he understood all about positions, so I would just pick 11 players who I thought were good enough to play. But, all of a sudden, I've started really getting into being a football manager. I thought I was like Alex Ferguson, and I was walking around telling off my players! One day, we were playing this team and we were winning about 15-0. I think the team just wanted to keep me happy, so they said to me, 'Coach, do you want to come on?' So I said, 'Yeah,' and I got all excited. I went out on that pitch and I was sliding about all over the place, but I managed to score a blasted goal!

In work, things were getting even better. I had started driving, delivering the filing cabinets to companies, which was great because it meant that I was out and about and I wasn't stuck in the factory all day. I used to put the filing cabinets in the van, check the delivery sheet to see where I had to go, and there were probably about five deliveries a day. I was going into all these posh offices up the West End and taking these cabinets in. I used to be in charge of the van keys and, to me, it was freedom. Also, my wages went up to £1 an hour.

They gave me a brand-new Luton van to drive around in, but it didn't have a radio in it. So I asked the manager if they could put a radio or a cassette player in it and he told me, 'If you keep the van for a month without damaging it, I will get you a radio.' Anyway, the same bloody week, I was doing a three-point turn in Camberwell Green and I knocked down a tree. Somebody took the number of the van and they got in touch with the manager, and he says to me, 'James, you knocked down a tree in Camberwell Green.' I told him that I didn't see the blasted tree, and the thing was they loved me in that company because they all used to come and watch me boxing. So my manager didn't make a big fuss, and I pretty much got away with it.

About a week after that, I was driving through the Blackwall Tunnel. I was singing away to myself and thinking about the fact that I had a boxing match coming up. I was thinking about what I was going to do and I was shadowboxing behind the steering wheel, and all this kind of thing. The Blackwall Tunnel is split into two halves, which separates the cars and the vans. So, there I am in my own little world, ducking and diving when I should have been thinking about driving, when, all of a sudden, I looked up and I saw the bloody pole that divides the tunnel into lorries and cars. I pretty much managed to miss it, but it just caught the top of the van as I drove through and it made a bloody great big hole in the roof.

When I got through the tunnel, I pulled over and I looked at this van with this bloody hole in it, and I thought, 'Oh, my God, I'm gonna get *killed* by my manager.' I went back to work late because I thought that, by five o'clock, everybody would have gone. But, as I reversed the damn van into the yard, all the managers were just leaving. I thought, 'What the hell are they doing here so late?' So I was smiling away and saying hello to all of them, and all I was doing was trying to lock up quick and get the hell out of there. The next day, the manager looked at the hole in the van and he called me inside the office. He did tell me off a little bit, but he *still* presented me with the damn radio.

They were a great bunch of guys that I was working with and, all in all, I was happy with the world. Work was good. Life with Carmen was great. I was 23 years old, and I knew that the time had arrived to take my next big step in the boxing journey of my life.

THE PROFESSIONAL

SHORTLY after Lisa was born, I decided that if I could get paid for boxing, that was the way for me to go. After being in the amateurs and having such great people looking out for me, I thought that I was grounded enough to know what it would be like turning professional. From the point of view of my fighting style, Jimmy and Ronnie used to teach me all the way along how to turn and how to twist. As an amateur, I had learned to box very much in a professional sort of style and people used to say that they didn't know how I got away with it. So I honestly thought that turning pro was going to be easy.

When I was boxing as an amateur, I had been pretty much doing it for fun. The pro game is a different thing entirely. To be honest, I didn't understand anything about professional boxing and how it all worked. But, when you turn pro, that is when it *really* becomes hard. There were so many good fighters around at the time, and these guys were willing to *hurt* you because they were all out there trying to put food on the table for their families, just the same as I wanted to be doing. Also, there is the business side of boxing to contend with, because boxing is a business first and foremost and, if you don't have the right people behind you, you ain't going nowhere.

After I lost my second ABA final to Johnny Graham and Jimmy Redwell said to me that, if I was going to get robbed, I might as well get paid for it, to be honest, I didn't really understand fully what he was getting at. I honestly believed that, once I got going as a professional, if I worked my way up through the ranks and kept winning fights, I would get on in my career and earn some good money. I had no idea about the politics of the boxing game.

When I finished with the amateurs, Jimmy Redwell said to me, 'Listen, James, I can't come with you. I would love to take out a pro licence myself and train you, but I can't.' Looking back on it now, I think the reason that Jimmy didn't want to come over into the pros with me was because he knew what the professional game was like and he didn't want to be part of that because, deep down, he knew that I would probably not get a fair ride and he probably wouldn't be able to do anything about it. That is the harsh reality of the boxing business.

When I turned professional, I don't think people ever really expected me to achieve anything. It was only guys like Johnny Graham who were picked as future champions, and that was because they were the ones who got signed up by the big managers with all the power. These guys got the big write-ups in the press and everything else, but I didn't really get any of that. When I went pro, they just said in *Boxing News*, 'He's a good puncher. Look out for him.'

Now that I understand the boxing game, I understand why even great amateur boxers don't always make it as professionals, because the work is very hard and having talent is one thing but, if you are not willing to put in that work and dedication, it is not going to happen. I was always out running, always in the gym training, always putting the work in to be the fighter that I wanted to be, and I think that is probably what brought me through as much as anything, which was just as well because I definitely didn't start out with one of the big managers.

I knew a gentleman called Al Hamilton who used to write for *The Voice* newspaper, and I was speaking to him about my boxing one day. He told me, 'There is a guy in Hackney named Billy Wynter who is managing fighters. You should go and see him.' It turned out that Billy Wynter was managing a fighter named Chris Christian, who fought Herol 'Bomber' Graham for the British light-middleweight title. At the time, I never even thought about shopping around to see what other managers were out there. I just went straight to see Billy Wynter because, now that I had made up my mind to become a pro fighter, all I wanted to do was to get started.

So that is when my professional boxing career began. I had my first professional fight in October 1982, and I carried on boxing for nearly 12 years before my time in the ring was over. I ended up having four different managers in total, and I gave them all three years of my life. But my first manager would be Billy Wynter.

BILLY WYNTER

BILLY Wynter originally came from Antigua and he had boxed professionally over here as a heavyweight in the Sixties and Seventies. Billy lost more fights than he won, but he had shared the ring with men like Richard Dunn, Danny McAlinden, Bunny Johnson and Joe Bugner, and he rarely got stopped.

When I first got to know Billy, I got a bit of a shock because, in those days, I naturally thought that managers had to be smart. I thought that a boxing manager would be in a suit, dressed up like a banker or something. But Billy was far from that. Billy was a down-to-earth sort of man who worked in the market. He used to come to the gym in his tracksuit, or whatever he was wearing, and he used to say, 'I don't have to wear a suit to be a manager.'

So I signed a contract with Billy Wynter, and Billy sent off to the British Boxing Board of Control to give them all my details and get my licence to fight sorted out. Billy wasn't one of the big, big managers or anything like that, but Billy was all right. He was a cool guy. The way he tended to work would be, if somebody came to the gym and said, 'We want James Cook to box,' then Billy would probably make the fight. Billy automatically thought that I could beat anybody anyway, and that was fine by me because so did I.

The first thing that Billy did was put me together with a trainer, a man called Brian Lawrence. Brian was older than me by about four or five years. He had boxed as a professional, but I think the reason why Brian quit was because they used to phone him up at short notice and he never had time to prepare himself properly. So Billy sent Brian off to get his professional trainer's licence and Brian became my first trainer.

Right from the start, I would say that me and Brian worked very well together because we both understood what was needed. Me and Brian would sit down and we'd work on things together, but I was secure enough in my style not to need too much technical input from Brian, and Brian realised that. I had already learned all the tricks of the trade that you need to survive as a professional from Jimmy Redwell and Ronnie White. If I was matched to fight somebody, Brian would look at them and, if we saw anything that I needed to be working on, we would work it into our training sessions. For instance, Brian might say, 'Watch the way he throws his left hook,' and then we would go to the gym and practise a particular right-hand counter punch. But, when me and Brian got together, it was mainly the fitness that we used to focus on.

Brian was a bloody good runner. When we'd go running in the mornings, we used to do ten miles and I used to have trouble keeping up with him because Brian was very competitive. When I used to run, I would always start off slow. So I would be going along in my own sweet little time, and Brian would be off like a rocket.

I will never forget the time when me and Brian parked the car at the Elephant & Castle and did a ten-mile run around Dulwich and back to the Elephant. By the time we reached halfway to Dulwich, I was thinking that I should really be making ground on Brian by now, so I was getting faster and faster. By this time, I was really into my zone, but Brian was still nowhere in sight. So I said to this lady at the bus stop, 'Excuse me, did you see somebody just run past here?' The lady said she hadn't seen anybody. So I carried on running to the next bus stop and I asked another two people if they had seen anybody run past there and they said they hadn't. So I was thinking to myself, 'How bloody fast is he travelling?' Then, when I was running up Dog Kennel Hill, there was a bus in front of me and, as I ran past the bus, I happened to turn around to have a look. That was when I saw Brian going past on the bus looking out of the bloody window! So I've raced the bus straight down to the Elephant & Castle and, when Brian got off the bus and ran across the road, I was not far behind him. I can't remember exactly what I said to him at the time, but I'm pretty certain that I called him a wanker.

My first pro gym was the Wellington in Highgate, which I am sad to say is actually a petrol station now. Apart from Billy Wynter's fighters, there were also a lot of Mickey Duff's fighters there and there was a lot of Darkie Smith's fighters in there too, both of whom would go on to manage me in future years, and the gym was always buzzing.

John Conteh used to train at the Wellington, and one of the things about John was that he used to do a lot of singing. I used to think, 'Fucking hell, why is he singing so much?' But, if you'd have seen that damn shower, it was so bloody cold in that shower, and I think that was why John used to sing inside the shower, to take his mind off the coldness. Also, I have got to be honest and say that John did have a great singing voice. We all used to look up to John inside the gym, but we never used to sing along with him because we never had good voices like him. There was only one single shower at the Wellington, and you had to wait for people to use it before you got your turn. The thing was, if John had a shower, he may use up all the hot water. So, after John had been in there, we used to time people while they were in the shower and we only used to get a couple of minutes each in there.

There were these little groups of us in the gym, all with our different managers and trainers, and we were all doing our own thing. So one of the very good things about the Wellington was there were all different sizes in there, so many fighters of different weight classes, and nobody was afraid to spar with anybody. You sparred with everybody and you learned from everybody. It was the toughness of sparring with these guys that brought me through and prepared me for my career as a professional fighter.

Prince Rodney was somebody who I sparred with regularly. Prince was British light-middleweight champion, and he was a very classy boxer and a bloody good fighter. But the problem with Prince was that he was very sneaky when you were in the ring with him. I learned a lot about chucking the uppercut when I was sparring with Prince Rodney because, when we used to get close on the inside, Prince would catch me with a crafty little uppercut that would get me a bit angry. Then, when I would go to react, Prince used to hold me and he would say, 'Cool, cool, cool, we're only sparring.' He used to do that to me all the time. Every time I tried to be aggressive and retaliate, Prince used to just have this way of calming me down. When I finally got to understand what he was doing, I just let loose on him. I wasn't going to let him do that to me too often, but this was after a good bloody six months of sparring with him.

One of the hardest punchers in the gym was John 'The Beast' Mugabi, who came over to London from Uganda to box for Mickey Duff. John was just starting out as a pro at around the same time as I was, and he went on to become world light-middleweight champion. The first time I saw 'The Beast' walking into the gym, somebody said to me, 'Do you want to spar with him?' They said to me, 'He's only 11 stone.' So I said, 'No way!' So they put John on the scales and he was 11 stone, so I said I would spar with him. Obviously, I had no way of knowing that John would turn out to be one of the best and, the first time that he hit me with his left hook, I thought, 'Fucking hell!' As soon as he hit me, I learned very quickly to do the rope-a-dope! But everybody that Mugabi sparred with came out of the gym hanging their head, because he used to just punch them so hard. John would come at you as if he was trying to take your head off.

John Mugabi was a real character and you never knew what he was going to do next. I will always remember this one time when he was talking in the corner with Mickey Duff, Dennie Mancini and George Francis, and John says, 'Can I have some money?' So Mickey said, 'Give him £25.' So John said to Mickey, 'No, no, no, I want *real* money.' So Mickey says, 'Give him an extra £25.' So John says, 'No, no, no, I want *real* money!' Anyway, in the end, they gave him £100. The next day, John was in the gym with a suitcase full of whiskey and cigarettes, and Mickey Duff was going bloody mad. Mickey was saying, 'I *told* you not to give him so much money!" That was so funny.

If I wasn't sparring at the Wellington, Billy Wynter used to take me down the Colvestone gym in Hackney, which was run by a funny little guy called Harry Griver. Harry was a black cab driver, and they used to call him 'Griver the Driver'. The Colvestone gym was a mixture of amateurs and professionals, and there were guys training there such as Michael Watson, Kirkland Laing and Dennis Andries.

Dennis Andries was a real tough guy. He was hard as nails and you could only do so many rounds with Dennis. I mean, I was young and fresh but, the longer Dennis went on, the more dangerous he became. The first time I sparred with Dennis, I said to Brian Lawrence, 'Let me do a six-round session with him.' Brian just looked at me as if I was mad and he said, 'Are you sure?' because Brian knew Dennis.

So me and Dennis got in the ring to spar and, in the first round, Dennis was missing me by miles. But, by the third round, his shots were only just about missing me. His fists were whizzing right past my bloody beard. So I said, 'Yeah, okay, that's enough now!' I had realised that, the longer he was going, the stronger he was getting as he was getting warmer, but I was getting tired. Sparring with Dennis taught me that a boxing match is not a three-round sprint. It gets harder and it gets tougher. It was easy to see why they called Dennis Andries 'The Hackney Rock', and the fact that he won the British title and became a three-time world light-heavyweight champion says it all.

The only pro who I probably didn't spar with at the Colvestone gym was Kirkland Laing, who was an outstanding welterweight. They used to call him 'The Gifted One'. I think the reason that we never sparred was because either Kirkland would turn up too bloody late or he would be gone by the time I arrived. But I know that Kirkland was a terrific runner because, when we used to run around the Hackney Marshes, you could hear him coming up behind you and then he would go flying past you, and all you could do was just wave to him, 'Hello, Kirk. Goodbye, Kirk.'

Kirkland Laing was such a brilliant boxer, but he had big problems when it came to self-discipline. There was another gym in Hackney that we used to call the Ghetto, and there were a few of us who used to use it. I remember one time, it was just after Kirkland had been out to Detroit and beat Roberto Duran, and Kirk rang me up and he said, 'Jimmy, have you got a key for the Ghetto gym?' So I said, 'Yeah, meet me up the gym.' By this time, Kirk was driving around in a white BMW. So I was walking up the road towards the gym and I saw this white BMW, and I could see all this smoke inside it. I didn't want to be too obvious about it, but, as I was walking past, I just sort of looked sideways into the car, and that was when I saw Kirk was sitting in the driver's seat. I said, 'Kirk, what are you doing? What is all this smoke?' So Kirkland says to me, 'Jimmy, it's just a little puff, just a little puff.'

I made my professional debut in October 1982. I was still working at the sheet metal place then. It was about lunchtime and I had been sitting out in the van when Billy Wynter phoned me up and said, 'You're fighting tonight at the Lyceum Ballroom in the Strand.' So I said, 'Who am I fighting?' I have to say I was really shocked when Billy told me that I would be fighting a chap called Mick Courtney. The thing was that me and Mick Courtney were friends, because Mick was in the Wellington gym as well. Mick was in there with Darkie Smith. I said to Billy, 'But he's my mate. Me and Mick Courtney spar together.' So Billy Wynter said to me, 'Are you going to let your sparring partner *beat* you?' I was so stunned. I think that was when I realised that this boxing game is tough and it doesn't care. In the boxing business, certainly back in those days, if your *mother* was a boxer and she was the same weight as you, you may have to fight her. So that was my welcome to professional boxing.

I won a points decision against Mick Courtney over six rounds, but to be honest it didn't feel good because we were gym mates. I wasn't really happy because he wasn't a stranger to me. He was a guy who I laughed with and spoke with all the time in the gym, and I didn't know whether I really wanted to hurt him or whether he really wanted to hurt me. It didn't feel exciting because I had sparred with him so many times. I knew that Mick was very tricky. I knew it wasn't going to be an easy fight. I knew he was tough, but I also knew that I had the boxing ability to beat him. On the other hand, this was my first fight without an amateur vest on, and Mick had already had four pro fights. So Mick knew what to expect and I didn't, but I knew I had to try and do enough to get a win.

I don't know how to explain it, but for some reason it didn't feel *real* fighting Mick. I remember putting him down, and I think he put me down as well. I came away with the win on my record and I *did* celebrate, but not as much as I would have if it had been a stranger who I had been boxing. But there were never no hard feelings between me and Mick, and we are still in touch to this day.

My next fight was just two weeks later. I boxed a Welshman called Gary Gething, and I fought him at one of the hotels in Piccadilly. I felt a lot better in that fight because I didn't know Gary Gething. My left hook and my right uppercut were two of my best punches, and I used them both that night and stopped him early in the second round. Because Gary Gething was a stranger to me and I was a stranger to him, I celebrated that victory a lot better than I did the Mick Courtney fight. The fight against Gething felt more like a proper professional win, and it was great for me to get the stoppage as well, because

I don't think people realised that I carried so much firepower and it was nice to show that off.

It was at this time that I made the decision that I wanted to just be a professional fighter and nothing else, so I packed in my job delivering the filing cabinets. As far as I was concerned, a man only needed to have one profession. I was now a professional boxer, so I wanted being a professional boxer to pay my living and I expected that to be the way it would work out. I wanted to train like everybody else. I wanted to train like John Conteh.

Being a professional, you expect to have money. You are walking down the road and you are telling people that you're a professional fighter. But unless you are at the top level and you're earning enough money to keep you and your family, being a professional don't mean nothing really. When you are just starting out on the road as a pro fighter, it is impossible to make a decent living at it unless you have been a big amateur star with people with money to back you and sponsors to help you. But that was something that I would find out soon enough.

My next fight was six weeks later, and I went to Birmingham to box a fella named Paul Shell in front of his home crowd at the Metropole Hotel. Obviously, the place was full of his fans, but I wouldn't say that they were horrible. I think they were just as normal fans would be. They wanted their man to win, but they weren't all that bad. Being the away fighter didn't bother me at all. All I knew was there was only two of us inside the ring and it was me and Paul Shell in there, not me and all of his fans. I always wanted to be the man who came out on top, and I ended up beating Paul Shell on points over eight rounds. So I came away from Birmingham with another win on my record, which was fine by me.

A month later, I experienced my first loss as a professional fighter. I was matched up to box a six-rounder with a fella named Jimmy Price, who was from Liverpool. Jimmy Price was a double ABA champion and he had won the Commonwealth gold medal. He had just turned pro with Frank Warren, who was really just coming into his own as a manager in those days. We boxed at the Crest Hotel in Bloomsbury and I don't know what the score was in the end. They gave him the decision, but I didn't think that he won the fight. When the result came, I thought it could have been a draw, at least.

Jimmy Price was a southpaw, but I didn't mind boxing southpaws. Once I was in the groove, it didn't make no difference to me what they were. So I have to say that I was seriously pissed off when Jimmy Price beat me the first time I boxed him, but I got over that. What *really* shocked me was when I boxed Jimmy Price again a year and a half later and he went and bloody *stopped* me. But I will come on to that in a little while.

A month later, I boxed Willie Wright from Birmingham at the Civic Hall in Solihull and I beat him on points. Willie was a tough guy, and he was funny because he kept on bloody talking to me all the way through the fight. In the first round, he was saying to me, 'Is that all you got, Cook? I nearly got you, Cook. This ain't no good, Cook.' This was the first time that I had ever come across a man who wanted to speak to me at the same time as I was fighting him, and I went back to my corner at the end of the round and I said to Billy Wynter, 'Billy, he's *talking* to me,' and Billy said to me, 'Didn't you know that he's a lunatic?' Apparently, that fight was initially supposed to be an eight-rounder, but then they cut it down to six. After it was over, Willy Wright says to me, 'A couple more rounds and I would have got to you, Cook!'

In those early stages of my career, Billy Wynter was getting me out boxing about once a month. In April 1983, I was matched up to box Dudley McKenzie at the Festival Hall in Basildon. When I was delivering the office equipment, Dudley's brother, Duke, worked for the company that used to spray-paint the filing cabinets. Me and Duke had made our pro debuts within a month of each other, and he had become a good friend who I liked to speak to. When the fight with Dudley was made, I said to Duke, 'You know that I'm fighting Dudley and I hope we can still be friends afterwards, despite what happens.' Duke said, 'Yeah, James, don't worry. Boxing is boxing, and we'll still be friends, no matter what the result.'

Dudley had slick skills and, believe me, at that time I think Dudley was probably the best fighter out of all the McKenzie brothers. But I ended up beating Dudley on points. Duke was there, but that was fine because, in those days, I think Duke understood the game a lot better than I did. For one thing, Duke had three brothers who were boxing and, for another thing, Duke was destined for greatness from the start. He was managed by Mickey Duff and he went on to become British, European and world champion. So, to be honest, Duke had a different sort of insight into the way the boxing business worked to most of us. Even though I had beat his brother, I think I was more upset about it than Duke was. But, after boxing Mick Courtney in my debut, I had learned early on that anything can happen in boxing. As for Dudley, he was like all of his brothers, a very brave fighter, but he never boxed again after he fought me.

One day, we were in the Wellington gym and Maurice Hope was in there. Maurice had been an outstanding fighter. Like Billy Wynter, Maurice came from Antigua originally, but he settled in Hackney and went on to win the British, Commonwealth, European and world light-middleweight titles. He had not long retired from boxing himself and was now managing fighters, so that was how me and Maurice came to know each other personally. At that time, Maurice was managing fighters like Prince Rodney and a heavyweight from Catford named Hughroy Currie, who went on to win the British title. Maurice also managed a middleweight from Manchester called Eddie Smith. Anyway, Maurice was speaking to Billy Wynter in the gym and, all of a sudden, they made a match for me to fight Eddie Smith. They made that fight on a bloody handshake, and I didn't know who the hell Eddie Smith was. I definitely didn't know how good or how tough Eddie Smith was.

There was a featherweight in the Wellington gym named Clyde Ruan, who was being trained by a tall man with white hair named Jim Warner. Jim was a great guy. He was one of those fellas who might be in the gym with his own fighter, but he would also take an interest in the other fighters and give them good advice. So, when I was doing my groundwork for the Eddie Smith fight, for about two weeks Jim Warner used to walk by and he used to say, 'Jimmy, make sure you do loads of groundwork because Eddie Smith is a bloody good body puncher.' So that was when I started to seriously increase my groundwork to fight Eddie Smith.

The fight took place at the Kings Hall in Manchester in May 1983. I boxed Eddie Smith the day before my 24th birthday, but that meant nothing to me. I just wanted to fight. I had a Mark 1 Granada at the time, and I drove it up to Manchester. There was me, Billy Wynter, Brian Lawrence and Lenny Lee in the car. Lenny was the corner guy who used to hand up the stool. He didn't used to train me, but most of the time he would be in my corner. Lenny was a lovely guy. He was very knowledgeable about boxing and he was just there inside the gym, and all he wanted was to be involved in what was going on.

Anyway, we were on our way to Manchester and the car only got a blasted puncture. So we pulled over on to the hard shoulder and I left the other three and went off to try and find a tyre somewhere. I ran down to the next exit and I found a garage at the top of the slip road where a guy told me that there was a breaker's yard around the corner. I found the breaker's yard and I managed to buy a tyre, and then I jogged all the way back to the car with this bloody tyre. We didn't care about motorway rules back then, and I can still remember Lenny Lee laughing as I appeared, running towards them and holding this bloody tyre out in front of me. Because of all the aggro, we turned up for the weigh-in very late and the promoter wasn't very happy. He said something to Billy Wynter about it, and Billy just looked at him and said, 'Do you want me to make the impossible possible?' Billy had a way of calming a situation down by the way he used to speak to people. He was great like that.

It was a good thing that I listened to Jim Warner's advice about doing my groundwork, because I don't think I knew what a bloody body punch was until I fought Eddie Smith. Before that, I had never really been hurt with a body shot in boxing because, as amateurs, we used to do a lot of groundwork anyway. But Eddie Smith was the only fighter I knew who chucked so many body punches. I could see why certain fighters focused on body shots because, in the end, no matter what, your stomach only can take so much. The first two rounds, I was dancing around and picking my shots and then, in the third round, I came out with my elbows superglued to my stomach! Eventually, I wore Eddie Smith down and I ended up stopping him in the sixth round.

On the trip home from Manchester that night, we stopped off in a petrol station so that I could put £25 worth of fuel in my Granada. The bloke behind the counter asked where we had come from and we told him that we'd been at the boxing show. He asked me, 'How did Eddie Smith get on, mate?' I said, 'He lost.' He says, 'Who beat him?' I said, 'I did,' and he says, '*Take* the fucking petrol, mate!' A lot of people didn't expect me to beat Eddie Smith, but I did beat him and I also got my tank filled up free at the petrol station, so that was a sweet drive back to London.

After the Eddie Smith fight, don't ask me why, but I just couldn't get any fights. It was very frustrating. When I was fighting, it wasn't for big wages. I was probably getting about £300 or £400 for a fight. Then all your expenses have to come out of that. I knew that I had to keep training so that, even if a short-notice fight came along, I would be fit and ready. But no fight came and, after fighting seven times in eight months, I didn't get out again for over six months. The only way for me to get a bit of extra money was to go out sparring with people for pay.

One of the men that I sparred with on a good few occasions was Mark Kaylor of West Ham. Me and Kaylor used to spar over at the Royal Oak gym in Canning Town, where there used to be Terry Lawless and Jimmy Tibbs and all their fighters, Frank Bruno and people like that. Mark was the one I was going there to work with, but I would also get in the ring with some of the others and I used to always hold my own. They weren't going to bash me up or try and bash me up and, even if they *did* try it, it never happened because I wouldn't let it happen. It was just good sparring and, if I sparred with them, it would probably make them fight a bit sharper and make them fight a bit more alert, because I wasn't the type of guy to just stand there and get hit.

Me and Kaylor never had any problem with each other. I got on well with Mark. He never said a bad word to me, and I never said nothing bad to him. I would go in there. We'd say hello to each other. We'd spar. We would have a chat when we were done, and that was it. He was paying me to get in the ring with him, and it was simply a matter of business for us. Mind you, although me and Mark were friendly outside of the ring, I knew that, by the time we touched gloves before the start of a sparring session, we were going to switch off the talking and concentrate on the job in hand.

One of the fights that Mark hired me to help him prepare for was when he challenged Roy Gumbs for the British and Commonwealth middleweight titles. I had also done some sparring with Roy Gumbs and, before the fight, somebody from the press phoned me up and asked me who I thought would win the fight, Gumbs or Kaylor. To be honest, I told them I thought that Gumbs would keep his titles, because he had that bit of skill where he touches and he moves, and things like that. I knew Mark Kaylor was tough, but I didn't think that Kaylor had that bit of slickness that was needed to outsmart Roy Gumbs. Once again, I think it was Jim Warner inside the Wellington gym who put me right when he turned around to me and said, 'Gumbs has got no heart.' So I said, 'What do you mean, he's got no heart?' Jim said, 'Once Kaylor gets on top, Gumbs will quit,' and he was right. Gumbs knocked Kaylor down, but Kaylor got back up and stopped Gumbs in the fifth round.

Billy Wynter finally got me another fight and I thought that, after six months out of the ring, they would probably give me an easy one to get me back into it, but no such luck! In November 1983, I went to box Vince Gajny at the Civic Hall in Solihull. Vince Gajny was a bit of a hard nut, I must admit. But I was just glad to get a fight to show everybody that I was still out there. It wasn't that I was really worried about the public forgetting about me. Nothing like that ever came to my mind. I think what was in my mind was that they thought they were going to get an unfit fighter who had been out of the gym and who hadn't been training and living right, but I was never that kind of man.

Vince Gajny was a light-heavyweight southpaw, so I was fighting above my natural weight, but that wasn't unusual and it didn't bother me. I was used to sparring with bigger people, so I wasn't really worried about weight or how big a man was. Before the fight started, I was looking across the ring at him and I was thinking, 'You are the same as me. You've got two arms and two legs, just like I have.'

I stopped Vince Gajny in the sixth round. To be honest, I think I broke his heart because, at the end of the round, he just turned to the referee and he said, 'That will do.' But the problem was that it wasn't only Vince Gajny's heart that got broke that night. I damaged my hand so badly during the fight that I was forced to take another six months out. That really put me back a lot, because it was a good win, but I couldn't get any momentum going to flow from that win, which was very disappointing for me.

By this point, I was starting to realise that there was no way that boxing was going to pay my living. I had thought that it would, but everybody makes mistakes and you learn these things as you go along. I never realised how hard it was to get fights without the backing of the right people who can move your career forward. There is a lot of disappointment involved in boxing. You go into it and you want the same thing as the next man. I was watching guys that I knew boxing on the television and doing well, and I was thinking to myself, 'They are not as good as me. Why are they on the TV? Why are they doing so well when I can't even get a fight?' It was very depressing.

When I think back to times like that, I have to give Carmen loads of credit because she put up with a lot. Sometimes, I was damn miserable, if you want to know the truth. Carmen didn't just put up with my moody periods while she kept our house and raised our kids. She went out to work every day as a hairdresser in a shop, and she also used to have clients who came to the house to get their hair done as well. Without the wages that Carmen was bringing into the house, I don't know how we would have managed. There were times when, if we were really struggling, Carmen's mum would help us out. She used to say, 'Son, have you got any money?' Then she would say to Carmen's dad, 'Give James £5 or £10,' and then Carmen's dad had to take the money out of his wallet. So it was a real blessing that there was always something coming in from somewhere.

I had never signed on the dole before, but somebody told me that I could make a claim, so I went down to Hackney Job Centre. I walked in there not having a clue what to expect, and this big black lady behind the counter shouted at me, 'Next! What do you want?' I will never forget that. I was thinking,

'Shit! I've only come down here for you to help me and now you are shouting at me like this.' Her attitude was so harsh that she made me feel like I was going there begging for money. So I just turned around and I walked straight out of there, and I never tried to bloody well sign on the dole again in my whole damn life.

About a week after my trip to the dole office, there was a riot around the Hackney area. It was all about the usual stuff. People in the area were struggling. They had nothing. The housing situation was bad and there was a lot of unemployment going on. These things used to happen and there was a lot of damage done around the place. There was a lady named Miss Anderson and Carmen used to do her hair, and she was the manager of an organisation called the Clapton Park Play Project. Miss Anderson told us that, because of the riot, they were looking for people who worked with kids and who understood kids. So I got a job with them and I was based in Hackney. I was a senior play worker, so I used to run after-school clubs, play projects and play schemes, and it was the sort of job that was right up my street.

A little while after that, I was asked to go for an interview with the Rathbone Foundation, which also operated here in Hackney. With Rathbone, it was just like what I had been doing before but on a much bigger scale. I think, during the time that I worked for Rathbone, I must have brought probably over 600 kids from around the area in off the street. The great thing about it was that, although I could bring them into the Rathbone offices, they also gave me the leeway to take the kids anywhere I wanted to and Rathbone would pay for everything. If some of the youngsters had had a hard night and I needed to take them to the café, I could buy them a meal and something to drink. If one of them happened to be going for a job interview, I could take them out and buy them the right clothes to make a good impression.

My project manager at Rathbone was named Aminul Hoque. Also, I had this great manager named Paul Fletcher, who was from Manchester. Because these guys trusted me and respected what I was doing, that gave me so much freedom. I spent a lot of my time out on the streets communicating with the young people, and I didn't have to clock in at nine o'clock or ten o'clock. I could get up and go in when I wanted. Some people who worked there didn't like it. They used to say, 'That Jimmy Cook comes in when he wants.' But I have never been the kind of man who goes to meetings. I have never been one to follow rules. I want everybody else to follow *my* rules. The most wonderful thing about being an outreach worker for Rathbone was that it gave me the time that I wanted to focus on my boxing training without any problems. So my future employment in youth work was firmly established, and that was what I did throughout the rest of my time as a professional boxer.

It was June 1984 before I was in the ring again. I challenged a guy named Tony 'T.P.' Jenkins for the vacant Southern Area middleweight title at the Royal Albert Hall. All I ever wanted was just to win a title as a professional, and the boxers in the mix for the Southern Area title in those days were a very tough bunch indeed. 'T.P.' Jenkins was an unbeaten Mickey Duff and Dennie Mancini fighter, and I knew that Mickey and Dennie wouldn't have a fighter unless he was very good and very capable.

   It was in this fight that all the sparring with guys like Dennis Andries, Prince Rodney and John Mugabi really paid off. It was sharing the ring with them which gave me the toughness that was required, and sparring with them also gave me the stamina I needed to be prepared to box for ten rounds. Because I had never boxed ten rounds before, I was probably losing a few of the earlier rounds against 'T.P.' because, in my head, I was thinking, 'I have got to box careful because this is ten rounds. I can't go out there and do nothing silly.' I was trying to be cool in the sense of saving myself for boxing, but trying to box to win the rounds, trying to use controlled aggression, rather than me going out there trying to knock 'T.P.' out and tire myself out in the process. Anyway, I put him down in the sixth and twice more in the ninth round, and then Harry Gibbs stepped in and stopped the fight.

   After I won the Southern Area title, I felt like I was on top of the world. The victory was even sweeter to me because it was a Mickey Duff and Dennie Mancini fighter that I beat. When you were boxing one of their fighters, it was 60 to 40 most of the time that they were going to beat you. Also, with 'T.P.' being previously unbeaten as well, I was really buzzing. The icing on the cake was the fact that this was my first professional fight at the Albert Hall. It was the first time I had been there since I lost the ABA final to Johnny Graham three years earlier, and to box there on a Mickey Duff show was great for me. As if all that wasn't enough, the fight was also considered as an eliminator for the British middleweight title as well. So it really was a great feeling that I had that night.

After all the excitement and happiness that went with winning my first professional title, my next fight brought me right back down to earth with a big thump. In September that year, I boxed bloody Jimmy Price again, this time at Wembley Arena. When I first turned professional, I never thought that I would be fighting somebody twice. I thought that, once you fought somebody, then that would be it and you could move on to the next person. I didn't realise that you could fight the same person ten bloody times.

This time, Jimmy Price stopped me in the second round. I was knocking him all over the place, and then I went in for a shot and bang! He caught me cold, and that was it. To be honest, whenever I think back to that fight, it still upsets me even to this day. That loss was more shocking to me than anything because, as a fighter, if somebody beats you and you don't think they should have beat you, revenge comes to your mind pretty strong. You want to make sure that you do the job properly if you ever get another chance. So I suppose that all I was thinking when I boxed Jimmy Price the second time was that I really wanted to stop him and get my own back for him beating me on points the last time. I wasn't thinking about the fact that he was a southpaw. I thought my hands were better than his, I thought my shots were faster than his and, when he knocked me out in the second round, I was absolutely devastated.

I had never been stopped before, not in the amateurs or the pros, and he actually knocked me right out. I remember chucking a punch and he went against the rope. Then, as I went in to capitalise, he chucked his left hook, or whatever he chucked, and it was game over for me. To be honest, because I had never been knocked out before, I don't know if it was in my head that I *couldn't* be knocked out or I *couldn't* be stopped, because I had never really thought about being stopped or getting knocked out. I just used to think that, once a fight started, I was still going to be there at the end. So, when Jimmy Price did that to me, it was definitely a big blow in more ways than one.

When something like that happens to you, particularly when it happens for the first time, it feels very bad when you are coming out of the ring and you're seeing all these people looking at you, and you're wondering, 'What are they thinking?' I was thinking about all these people seeing me getting knocked out and, for me, it was more of an emotional pain than a physical pain. I was thinking about letting people down, walking past this crowd and them believing that I was no good, that I was rubbish. You have to walk back through the arena and all those people are there, and it's like you weren't good enough. To make matters worse, that fight was a final eliminator for the British title. Afterwards, I was so annoyed with myself because I felt that, by this stage of the game, I should have known better than to get caught the way that Jimmy Price had caught me, and I couldn't face nobody. I couldn't even face myself. I felt so ashamed.

I left the arena and I jumped in my car. I drove around the West End until my car ran out of petrol, and then I just left the damn car on the side of the road. I got out and I started to walk and, all of a sudden, this old boy stopped me in the street. I don't know where he came from, but I think he was probably one of these old boys who was at the fight. He just stopped me and he said to me, 'Cook, in this game, if you can't take losing with winning, you shouldn't be in the game.' When I sat down the next day and thought about what the old man had said, that gave me the strength in my mind to pick myself up and go again. Whoever that old boy was, he is still there as part of my life. I only wish that I could remember what he looked like. After that, every time I lost a fight, I would go back to the gym and I would just work harder and harder. Basically, every loss I experienced after that, I would hear the voice of that old boy, and the words he said to me that night have always stuck with me.

After that second loss to Jimmy Price, it was eight months before another fight came along, but thankfully there were always sparring jobs to be had as something to fall back on. It was during this time that I went up to Leicester to spar with Tony Sibson when he was preparing to box Mark Kaylor for the British, Commonwealth and European titles, and I have to say that Tony Sibson is the only bloody man who ever completely outran me. I was upset, because Tony was stockier than me and he took me for a bloody run and he left me. To make matters worse, at the end of the run, when I got back to the gym, there was Tony chopping this blasted tree up!

Until I sparred with Tony Sibson, I never knew that black men could get black eyes. When we went to the press conference, Mickey Duff pointed to my eye and he said, 'That is Tony's left hook working,' because Tony was a good left hooker. So working with Tony Sibson was a hard job, but he was a lovely guy and we had a lot of laughs together. Also, it kept the money coming in, which was just as well because our daughter, Keisha, came along the following month and the Cook household was getting bigger.

My first fight of 1985 took place in May at Portchester Hall in the Queensway, London. I was defending my Southern Area title, and in the other corner was Conrad Oscar. I never had the kind of manager who would say, 'Okay, you just got knocked out by Jimmy Price, so we will ease you back in.' It was straight on to Conrad Oscar, who was as tough as hell. But I still remembered that headline when we were back in the amateurs when it said, 'After beating Cook, Oscar goes pro,' and I wasn't happy with that. So this was the only fight where I felt that I wanted to punish a fighter, like Muhammad Ali used to punish fighters.

During the fight, I was looking out at the people sitting at ringside, looking at Conrad, and then chucking punches. That is how confident I was that night. Although Conrad Oscar was rough and hard, I quickly realised that he could not hurt me. He wasn't as quick as me and I could handle whatever he was chucking at me. All I was thinking about was that he never really won that fight in the amateurs, and I beat him up for ten rounds. Also, Conrad Oscar was managed by Harry Holland, who would become another one of my managers further down the line. Harry had a company called Winners Worldwide, and he promoted the show live on BBC1. So I would say that, when I defended my Southern Area title against Conrad Oscar, that was one of my favourite victories up until that time in my career as a pro.

Five months later, I went to Birmingham to defend my Southern Area title against Tony Burke of Croydon, and I honestly didn't think he was going to be a problem. With me being the champion, before the fight I was thinking, 'Who is Tony Burke? Why did the Board give me Tony Burke?' I didn't know anything about Tony Burke. I didn't know whether he could punch or if he could fight. I didn't read about Tony Burke. All I knew was the British Boxing Board of Control said that I had to defend my Southern Area title against him.

I wouldn't say that I was overconfident. But, because I hadn't been thinking too much about Tony Burke and I had never even seen him, all I was thinking was that he shouldn't beat me. When I *did* see Tony Burke, I thought, 'Damn! He's got a lot of muscle.' He had muscle all over his body. He had muscles in his arms, muscles on his forehead, muscles in his eyes, and he was built like a tank! But, the way I was thinking, that muscle wasn't going to go ten rounds. I was thinking to myself, 'Once I get you past five rounds, then you're mine.'

In the first round, I was rocking Tony Burke all over the place. When I hit him the first time and he started to go, in my head I was thinking, 'Okay, I hit you, I've hurt you and you can't take a punch, so I'm coming in to hit you again.' That was when I got a bit cocky and I dropped my hands. Harry Gibbs was the referee for that fight and, as I was on my way back over to my corner at the end of the round, Harry followed me over and he said to me, 'Cook, keep your hands up, this boy can punch.'

Anyway, I went out for the second round and started all the flash stuff. I hit Tony Burke, and I think he went against the ropes and I dropped my hands to go in and finish him off. That is when Tony Burke hit me with the hardest right hand that you could ever be hit with and I fell straight down in the middle of the ring. The next thing I remember, I was looking up at Harry Gibbs, and he was looking down over me and I was expecting him to say 'One, two, three,' but he looked down at me and he said, 'Cook, I *told* you so!' So Tony Burke went and stopped me in the second round and I lost my Southern Area title.

When I was back inside the changing room, I think I was still in a bit of a daze because I was sitting there thinking, 'I kind of like Harry Gibbs. He tried to warn me and I didn't listen to him.' Harry didn't have to give me that advice and I thought that was nice of him. But, when the shock wore off and the reality of what had just happened hit me, it was sickening. I was devastated, and it took such a long time to get back into contention after that. When you get knocked out a couple of times or you get stopped a couple of times, you worry that people might start to lose faith in you.

My three-year contract with Billy Wynter had come to an end and nobody really told me to jump ship after the Tony

Burke fight. But I was thinking to myself, 'I'm up the gym and I'm not getting many fights.' Although Billy Wynter had a few fighters, I could see that Darkie Smith had a *lot* of fighters, and I thought I needed a manager with a lot of fighters. So, when the contract with Billy ran out, I decided that the time had arrived to make a change and I signed up with Darkie Smith.

DARKIE SMITH

THE day after I signed a contract with Darkie Smith, we were all sitting around in the Wellington changing room talking and I think it was Jess Harding, a heavyweight who was with Darkie, who said to me, 'Jimmy, did you sign a contract with Darkie?' So I said, 'Yeah', and all of Darkie's boys who were there burst out laughing. So I turned around to them and I says, 'What are you guys laughing at? Darkie is *your* manager. Why shouldn't he be *mine*?' They said, 'No, Jimmy, Darkie is just our *trainer*, not our manager,' and I thought, 'Oh, shit!' So I don't know if I was actually the first fighter that Darkie Smith ever managed, but I was probably the biggest fighter that he managed.

The good thing about Darkie was that he took me abroad to box a lot of times, which I think toughened me up. I had five fights abroad in about a year and a half with Darkie, and I think I was chucked in the deep end. But I believe that it was the experience I got from boxing in these different countries that made me a man in the game of boxing. The toughness of going to fight a foreign fighter abroad hardens you. It gave me that durability and it made me more robust. It also ended up standing me in good stead for the future because, when I became a trainer myself when my own boxing career came to an end, when I had to go abroad with fighters, I knew what to expect.

My first fight with Darkie was in March 1986, when I went to Cologne to fight Graciano Rocchigiani, who went on to win world titles at super-middleweight and light-heavyweight after he boxed me. Rocchigiani was very flash and arrogant at the weigh-in, and it seemed like he had control over the people around him. His came in on the scales a bit over the limit, and he refused to get the weight off. I was thinking, as a fighter, if you are supposed to be boxing at a certain weight, you should always make that weight. But Graciano told them that he wasn't going to take the weight off and then he just walked away.

So now I was looking at my manager and I was thinking, 'Okay, Darkie is going to do something now,' because, if something like that happens, you look to your manager to say something, to be more active. I thought Darkie was going to stick up for me, but it never happened. Obviously, being over there, being a fighter, I had my family to think about now. I had missed work for a day to go over there and I wanted the money. So I decided to go ahead with the fight anyway. I did eight rounds with Graciano Rocchigiani and I lost on points, and that was my welcome to my first professional fight abroad.

Less than a month later, Darkie took me over to Amsterdam to box a Dutchman named Jan Lefeber. He was a natural light-heavyweight and he knocked me out in the second round. So that was the next great experience. I remember that fight so well. In the fight, he was like everybody else, rocking all over the place. But my rude awakening came when, after knocking him down, the referee came over and picked him up and turned him around. Then I dropped my fists and went in to shake Jan Lefeber's hand, and he fucking hit me! I went down, and the referee looked down at me and he said, 'Cook, I didn't officially call an end to the fight.' But I had never seen a referee pick a fighter up like that before. To me, once a referee holds you or picks you up, the fight should be finished. Once again, Darkie did nothing to stick up for me. Once again, it was a lesson to me. You learn that, when you are going abroad to box, you really need to have the right team around you who know what they are doing. You need people who really are in your corner. You need people who ain't scared to stick up for you.

To be honest, I don't actually remember the journey home from Amsterdam after the Jan Lefeber fight, but I do know that I wasn't happy with Darkie. I wasn't happy with him at all, but I kept quiet about it during the flight. I always kept a cool head, and I logged everything as experience in my life, just as I still do today, because that is what life is all about. I was never one to mouth off because everything is experience, so you learn as you go along.

The problem was that there was someone else who wasn't happy with Darkie by now, and that was my trainer, Brian Lawrence. I think that Brian was getting upset with Darkie because I don't think Darkie was talking to Brian enough and keeping him in the picture about what was going on. Because of the situation, Brian ended up leaving me after the Jan Lefeber fight. So Brian stayed out of the picture for a while and then he came back to me after I eventually left Darkie. But I couldn't get involved in all these disagreements. As a person, as a fighter, all I wanted to do was just train and fight.

When Darkie told me that I was going to be fighting Michael Watson, I was quite happy about it because I had been reading about Michael in the local press. They were shouting about how he was tough, and saying that he was tall and good looking, which upset me because I was thinking, 'Hell, no, there is *nobody* better looking than me in Hackney. We can't have two good-looking men in Hackney. I'm not having it!'

Also, I felt that I badly needed the sort of fight that would show people I wasn't just a journeyman travelling abroad and getting beat. To be really honest, I reckon that I needed to prove something to myself as well because the truth was that, in my mind, I was starting to have doubts. I was beginning to ask myself, 'Can I really fight?' After losing twice to Jimmy Price, the loss against Tony Burke, and losing the two fights abroad, I think my confidence was a little bit shaken.

Me and Michael Watson fought each other in May 1986 at Wembley Arena, and I beat him on points over eight rounds. Up until then, Michael had been undefeated in seven fights, so I became the first fighter to beat him as a professional. The thing was that Michael was with Mickey Duff in those days, and I think Mickey Duff probably saw my record, that I had lost four of my last five fights and I had been stopped three times, and Mickey probably thought that the time had come for Michael to beat me. In truth, it was the fact that I now had those losses on my record that spurred me on to beat Michael, and Michael was pretty tough. He was a hard man to shift, and I could easily see why he went on to fight for a world title.

After me and Michael boxed, we both used to train at the same gym in Finsbury Park and use the running track. But it was a while before we met up face to face again because one of us would turn up early or the other one would turn up late, and we kept missing each other. One day, we happened to bump into each other at the door and he said to me, 'Cook, what about a return?' I said, 'When you beat Chris Eubank, *then* we can have the return.'

A little bit further down the line, there was supposed to be a final eliminator for the British title. There was me, Michael Watson, Johnny Melfah and Herol 'Bomber' Graham all in the mix. By now, me and Michael had become good friends and he wasn't too happy about the thought of fighting me again. Even though I had a much bigger understanding by now of how these things happen in boxing, I think that, deep down, I was also glad that it never happened. Michael and I are still great pals and, these days, he always tells people, 'I can't believe that I let this old boy beat me, but I'm *glad* you beat me, old boy!' I always like to remind Michael that he ended up with a nosebleed and I didn't, so I was definitely the better-looking man at the end of the fight!

After I boxed Michael, I had to wait nine months before I could box again because Darkie was telling me that he couldn't get me any fights. But I still had my day job at Rathbone and I was still training two or three times a day. I was always in training while I was waiting for fights to come up. I used to get up at four o'clock in the morning and drive over to the Elephant & Castle to start my running. I would run my ten miles, come back and change for work. Sometimes, when I needed to ease down on the roadwork, I would just run from Hackney to Tottenham and back, and then I would go to the park and do my sprints.

I was never one of these guys who went off the rails in between fights. I never took up drinking or smoking because I still had a licence as a professional fighter. So, even if I wasn't fighting, I was still in the gym as a professional fighter, because I still believed that one day I was going to get there and be where I wanted to be. I have to admit that it was upsetting sometimes to see guys fighting regular while I was sitting around on the sidelines, especially when I knew that a lot of them weren't as good as me. I kept thinking, 'Why isn't that me? Time is passing me by.' I think that happens in any sport. There comes a point when you start to realise that it is not going to go on forever and, if you waste too much time, you are never going to get that time back.

Eventually, Darkie took me back out on the road again. In February 1987, we went to France and I fought an African fella named Mbayo Wa Mbayo. To be honest, all I really remember about that fight was that he spent the whole night bloody running from me and, in the end, they gave him the decision on points. It was just a normal fight abroad in the sense that, if I didn't knock him out, I was never going to get the result.

A month after the Mbayo fight, our daughter, Jamie, came along. I had to wait eight months before Darkie got me out boxing again, so I had to get back on to the sparring circuit to make a bit of cash. I held my own with anybody who wanted decent sparring, and I think the only one who I got hit by, or who made me get hit, was Herol 'Bomber' Graham. I went to a gym in Belfast to spar with 'Bomber' while he was preparing to defend his European middleweight title against Sumbu Kalambay at Wembley, and his trainers kind of forced me just to use my jab, because Kalambay had a good jab and that was why they wanted me. After sparring with Herol Graham with one hand, let me tell you that I was very sore afterwards, but that is just part of being a boxer. What stung me the most was the fact that I didn't think I was getting enough money for a job like that.

There was one time when I had been doing some sparring with Lloyd Honeyghan, and I definitely charged Lloyd £400 for my services. A week later, I saw Lloyd at the bus stop and I said to him, 'Lloyd, where is my money?' Lloyd said, 'Jimmy, I paid the money over to Darkie as soon as the sparring was done.' So I went straight back to talk to Darkie about it and, when I asked him where my money was, he was telling me that, because I had pulled out of a fight before, he had to pay for this and he had to pay for that.

For my next fight, Darkie took me over to Italy to box a fighter named Willie Wilson. Willie Wilson was a very strong

American and he was a regular sparring partner for the world welterweight champion, Donald Curry. I can't remember the name of Willie Wilson's manager, but apparently the fella was a bit of a loudmouth. As it happened, Larry O'Connell was also over in Italy because he was one of the judges for the fight on top of the bill. I knew Larry O'Connell well because he had refereed a few of my fights by this time, and I think he was a brilliant referee. Larry was a great mover, and he would sort of float towards you and then he would float back. Larry had a great way about him that made you respect him. He would always speak to you with a smile, but he was also honest and he was always firm with fighters when he was the referee.

The thing was I think that Willie Wilson's manager must have really pissed Larry off, because Larry came up to me before the fight and he said to me, 'James, if you can beat this American, I will be so happy because his manager hasn't stopped nagging me all day.' Apparently, Willie Wilson's manager had been talking non-stop to Larry, saying, 'I tell my fighters what to do and what to eat.' Larry said that the man hadn't left him alone and he was driving Larry mad.

When I got in the ring to fight Willie Wilson, I had been told that it was going to be an eight-round fight. The first few rounds were probably quite close, but I wasn't worried because I knew that I would come on strong later in the fight. But, when I went back to my corner after round five, Darkie said to me, 'James, they've changed it and it's a six-rounder instead of eight now.' So I asked, 'Will I get the same money?' Darkie said, 'Yes, it's the same money.' So I said, 'Okay, no problem,' and I went out for the sixth round and gave Willie Wilson a Jimmy Cook special, because by this time I was really developing my right uppercut. When I used to chuck that right uppercut, I wasn't chucking it for fun. When I was fighting, if I saw any sort of weakness in my opponent, I would be looking to throw that punch. I knew that, even if I didn't catch them with it properly, it would take something out of them. So I just hit Willie Wilson with it, and he was out like a light.

As soon as the fight was stopped, Larry O'Connell couldn't help himself. He jumped up out of his seat and he shouted out loud, 'Fuck the Americans!' Then Larry remembered that he was one of the judges for the main fight, and he had to sit back down a bit quick. That was such a funny thing to see and, after the fight, Larry was so happy. He hugged me and he said, 'James, I am *so* glad that you beat the American.' As for me I was over the moon about the victory because that was my first win abroad and it was a great feeling, especially because they were looking to big up Willie Wilson as this big American hot prospect, and I done a number on him. That was such a happy journey home.

A few weeks after I stopped Willie Wilson, I was matched up to box a fighter named Tarmo Uusivirta in Finland. Darkie told me that my purse money was going to be £1,500, which was fine by me until I heard a different side of the story. I was down the Wellington, and it was my old friend, Jim Warner, who told me the truth. Jim said to me, 'How much are you getting for this fight?' So I told him that I was being paid £1,500. Jim just smiled and shook his head, and he said to me, 'No, you're not. You're getting about three grand.' Jim Warner had never given me bad advice, and I knew that he was telling me the truth. I was starting to think about certain times when we had been at an airport together and Darkie would say, 'Don't worry, James, I will buy that for you.' By now, it was starting to occur to me that Darkie might have been buying me stuff with my own bloody money!

I became very angry and, a couple of days before the Tarmo Uusivirta fight, I started telling Darkie that I wanted more money. At first, Darkie was saying, 'No, James, you're not going to get no more money.' But I wouldn't leave it alone this time. I kept saying to him, 'Darkie, I want more money.' So eventually, Darkie came back to me and he says, 'Yeah, okay, they're gonna give you another £500.' As we were arriving at the airport, I says, 'Darkie, I want some more money,' and Darkie was going mad. His voice sounded like he was in pain. It was like I was trying to take one of his teeth out! He was going, 'Nah, you're *not* gonna get no more money!' In the end, when we got to the airport, Darkie went away screaming to himself, and then he came back and he says, 'This is it! You can have another £500, but they're *not* gonna give you no more!'

Tarmo Uusivirta was a big, blond Finnish fella and I boxed him in an indoor ice rink. He beat me on points and, at the end of the fight, I wasn't even sweating because it was so cold in there. It was such a close fight and I didn't believe that he beat me, and all I could hear was Tarmo's fans shouting, 'Cook, how is the weather?'

It was Tarmo's people who put on the promotion for that show, and they actually didn't want to pay me in the end. The thing was that there was no way that the ice rink was sold out, and I don't think they had made the money that they were expecting. Darkie was of no help whatsoever and, in the end, it was the bloody referee who sorted things out. He said to me, 'James, don't worry. Your money will be at the airport by the time you get there.' He was a foreign referee and I can't remember his name, but he was a great guy and, sure enough, by the time we reached the airport, the money was there.

My next fight was actually pretty easy compared to what I had become used to. I boxed a guy called Cliff Curtis, who was a journeyman from up north, at the Festival Hall in Basildon. When I fought Cliff Curtis, it never seemed as though I had to put up that much effort. Everything I was doing, it was what I wanted to do and how I wanted to do it. He was giving me the range to do what I wanted. It was nice work, and I stopped him in the fourth round. After the fight was finished, I thought to myself, 'Damn! Couldn't Darkie have got me more fights like this before?'

Two months later, I was back in action and this was a fight that I knew would be far from easy. The match was made for me and Herol 'Bomber' Graham to box for the vacant British middleweight title. Because I'd already had the experience of sparring with 'Bomber' in Belfast, I knew in no uncertain terms how good he was. So, after being told that I was going to be fighting him and with it being for the British title as well, this was the first time that I decided to go away and get myself a training camp. By now, we had the kids and I thought I would go away and try and get a bit of peace. I wanted to be able to go to bed early and get up early, and stuff like that. But I have to admit that I didn't go too far away. I moved out of our home in Hackney and went to stay with my Auntie Lovely, who lived at the Elephant & Castle and, every day after I had finished my roadwork, I would be running up the escalator at the Elephant tube station.

All I wanted to do was just focus on the fight, because obviously, it was Herol 'Bomber' Graham, so I couldn't train for him like normal. I was going in against probably Britain's finest boxer at the time and I was facing him in his hometown. He was the man that everybody was talking about. He was the man that everyone wanted to beat. I knew that 'Bomber' was very tricky. He was an awkward, switch-hitting southpaw. I knew that he had only lost once in 40 fights, and I knew that he had stopped a lot of fighters. All I was thinking was, 'If he *does* stop me, he ain't going to stop me early and, if I'm still there after that, then we will see what happens.'

Me and Herol 'Bomber' Graham boxed in June 1988 in Sheffield. I took a few people with me in a minibus and, when we arrived in Sheffield, all these people were coming up to me and saying, 'Who are you, coming here to fight our man?' Even after all the fights I'd had in foreign countries, this was the first time that I ever felt a little twinge inside my stomach, because so many people were looking at me with real hostility just because I was walking down the damn street.

When I stepped through those ropes in the Sheffield City Hall, the reception that the crowd gave me made me feel as if I was from bloody Germany, and his fans were so close to the ringside. The opening bell went and, in the first couple of seconds, 'Bomber' rushed at me and he threw me to the floor. The referee was Sid Nathan, and Sid gave 'Bomber' a stern warning about that. Then 'Bomber' went and put me down again before the end of the first round, but I can't say that I was really hurt.

I remember seeing Prince Naseem Hamed walking around the place, and he was obviously watching closely. Prince Naseem was still a young amateur boxer at the time, but he must have been a good judge even back then because I remember him shouting out, 'Watch the uppercut.' In fact, even now, whenever Prince Naseem sees me these days, he says, 'This is the man who chucks the most dangerous uppercut in the business.'

I have to admit that my fight with 'Bomber' wasn't an all-time classic and, in the end, Sid Nathan stopped it in the fifth round. 'Bomber' had come out with his hands dangling by his sides and I caught him with my right uppercut, but he just poked his damn tongue out at me! Then he wound up his right hand, Sugar Ray Leonard style, and he caught me with a cheeky left hook that cut my eye. I got put down one more time after that, and that was when Sid Nathan stopped the fight.

I have to say that, at the time, I was quite angry at Sid Nathan because I didn't like the fact that he stopped the fight when he did. He said it was because I was bleeding, but he never gave me no time to go back to the corner for them to have a look at the cut. He said that I looked a bit dazed, but I didn't *feel* dazed. At the time when the fight was stopped, I was just getting into it. But, at the same time, I must admit that there were moments during the fight when I saw 'Bomber' was doing this move or that move and I was thinking to myself, 'You can't make a move like that and hit me,' and then he *did* make that move and he *did* hit me. It was a bloody hard fight.

After any loss, you always feel bad. I remember that night, as I left the ring, I felt terrible because I felt like people were looking at me like I didn't try, like I wasn't supposed to be there, like he ran rings around me. I know that you can't do anything to change what has happened in the past. But, looking back on it now, I sometimes think I should have been more aggressive with 'Bomber'. When I went in for that fight, in my head, I was cool. I was thinking, 'We're going 12 rounds and I will catch you up. I'll take my time and I will pick you off in there, and I will get to you in the end.' I honestly wasn't expecting him to come out like a train and, if I'd have known what he was thinking and what he was going to do, I would have probably tried to be more rough with him. When I went into that fight, I truly believed that I was still going to be there at the end of the 12 rounds, but it turned out that I got that wrong.

But I have got to say that there were never any bad feelings between me and 'Bomber'. A few years after we boxed each other, we both ended up being managed by Mickey Duff. By that time, I was British and European champion, and me and 'Bomber' were doing some sparring together down at a gym in King's Cross. I remember it got quite heavy because I was thinking, 'Well, I can't fight you now, so let's get it on in sparring.' To be honest, I think that was when I finally got my own back during that sparring session, because I was up at that level now with him. All I remember was Mickey Duff screaming his head off. He was shouting, 'No! Stop it! You're not getting paid!'

Unfortunately, life has been very unkind to Herol and he has been having a big struggle with depression. I feel very sad that he is at such a hard place in his mind right now, because he was one of the greatest fighters in this country. Everybody wanted to be like Herol 'Bomber' Graham. Everybody wanted to dance like him, to move like him and to chuck punches like him. Herol knows that he was truly special, and he can't comprehend the way that his life has turned out.

It seems to me that, when a fighter is that special, the way that 'Bomber' was, it can hurt them later on in life. Sometimes, when you have too much talent, too much talent will bring you down. Sometimes, when there is too much talent, things just don't run smoothly, and I think 'Bomber' was one of these guys with too much talent. If you look at Gazza, Hurricane Higgins, George Best, Kirkland Laing, and even The Greatest himself, all of these guys with brilliant talent, for some reason things don't seem to end well for them. That is why I think it is so important to have friends around you who are natural and down to earth, no matter who you are. When you're a superstar like Herol 'Bomber' Graham and you lead that sort of life, when the time comes for it all to be over, people forget about you.

Herol is now in a position where he really needs looking after. Because he was so highly regarded in this country, I just expect more from the boxing fraternity. The promoters could help set something up for fighters. I do definitely think that all the promoters and managers who have made a lot of money should all get together and set something up for the fighters who ain't living a good life. These men have stepped into the ring and risked their lives to entertain us over and over again, and I feel that we should look after them if they fall on hard times.

When I fought Herol 'Bomber' Graham, I got paid £10,000. After my conversation in the gym with Jim Warner before the Tarmo Uusivirta fight, it made me wonder how much more that fight really might have been worth and, the way I was feeling, I knew that I had reached the end of the line with Darkie. There had been too many times when I had needed him to back me up and I didn't feel like he had ever done that for me. As for my suspicions about the money situation, I am happy to say that money was never my god because, if it had have been, then I think I probably would have killed a manager like Darkie Smith.

I think the reason that boxers don't beat up managers who they believe have robbed off them and treated them badly is because the majority of boxers tend to have respect for people. That is one of the reasons that boxing is the greatest sport in the world. You get upset with people, but you still have this respect. Another reason why I think some of these managers have always got away with doing some of the things they do is that, deep down, whatever break they give a fighter, the fighter will still find himself thanking his manager for it. Most fighters are just grateful for the work. But fighters have got to work so damn hard for their money and they have got families to feed as well. Nobody wants to kill their manager, but what we want them to be is more honest because, if they lie to us and cheat us and steal from us, that leaves a bad feeling.

My contract with Darkie had come to an end, and he was probably pissed off when he realised that I was leaving him. But Darkie knew what time of the day it was because he knew that, by this time, I had caught him out too many times. So, when I left Darkie, he never really made too much of a big thing about it. He definitely already knew that it was on the cards, because he came to see Carmen before the Herol 'Bomber' Graham fight, when I was staying at the Elephant & Castle with Auntie Lovely. He was trying to persuade Carmen to tell me not to leave him, but Carmen never said anything about it to me at the time. Afterwards, when I found out, I said to Carmen, 'You should have told me about it, and then I would have probably beat up Herol Graham over it!'

When all is said and done, I can't say that going with Darkie Smith was a complete mistake. I have never been the type of man to hold on to a grudge. I don't see the point in that because life is definitely too short. Darkie is out of my life now and I am still here to tell my story. My time with Darkie was a part of my boxing journey. Whatever else went down, it was an experience that made me a better fighter and, as far as I am concerned, that is all that matters.

My mum and dad.

With my childhood sweetheart, the love of my life and my beautiful wife, Carmen.

Sharing the ring at York Hall with Errol Christie in a fight that meant everything to both of us. In the end, I stopped him in five. [PA Images]

The new British champion posing for a publicity photo.

Chilling out at home with my Lonsdale belt.

Before my fight with Mark Kaylor, which was billed as two gentlemen having a cup of tea. [Michael Fresco]

Before I stopped Mark Kaylor in the sixth round at York Hall. It was a fight that came at the right time for me, because I still say that I would never have beaten the Kaylor of old. [Les Clark]

Mark Kaylor, brave to the end.

With my European belt after defending my title against Mark Kaylor, with Brian Lawrence and Harry Holland. [Getty]

Defending my European title against Tarmo Uusivirta at Latchmere Leisure Centre, and showing him that he was in my town now. Tarmo retired in the seventh round and it was sweet revenge for me. [Les Clark]

With my old pal, Frank Bruno.

On the way to the ring with Ian Napa. In his day, Napa was one of the most talented fighters in this country. [Philip Sharkey]

Taking Tommy Eastwood on the pads. Tommy was a tough man with a wicked sense of humour.

Racing sheep with Larry O'Connell and Colin McMillan over the Southwark Bridge.

Me and my dad before my wedding. In the background line-up are my brothers, my nephews, my grandson and the white guy is Ben Way, the secret millionaire. [Charlz Albert]

Carmen and I taking our vows. [Charlz Albert]

Catching a quiet moment with Michael Watson on the big day. [Charlz Albert]

Receiving my MBE from Her Majesty The Queen.

At Buckingham Palace with Lydia, Carmen and Lisa on one of the proudest days of my life.

My two sisters, Lydia and Angela, together with Evans.

Brothers in arms (Left to right: Simon, Brian, myself and Evans).

All dressed up with my wonderful family. I am indeed a very lucky man.

Being carried out of the ring by Derek Williams and Julius Francis at the opening of the Pedro Boxing Club.

HARRY HOLLAND

AFTER the loss against Herol 'Bomber' Graham, I was seriously thinking of calling it a day. When I first started out as a professional, the idea I had in my head was that I was going to quit this sport at the age of 30, whether I had won a title or not. I had already won the Southern Area title and I was 29 years old when I was stopped by 'Bomber'. So I was starting to think to myself, 'This is it. It's time to go.' But Carmen always had faith in me 110 per cent, and I will never forget her saying to me, 'James, listen to me. If boxing is what you want, then go and do what you need to do.' A lot of boxers have problems in their domestic lives because their missuses don't like them fighting. So that is how lucky I was, to have a woman as understanding and as loyal as Carmen.

One thing I had noticed was that, no matter where I was when I was out and about on the boxing circuit, the manager and promoter, Harry Holland, always went out of his way to say hello to me. I was feeling so low after losing to 'Bomber' and I felt like I couldn't talk to anybody about it. But then I thought about this man who would make time to say hello to me everywhere I went, and that is why I decided to give Harry Holland a call. I found his number in the British Boxing Board of Control Yearbook and I rang him up. I asked him if he thought I should retire, and Harry says to me, 'No, James, I think you are a good fighter still.' He told me, 'When I look through the ratings, you can still beat half of these guys and I think you can definitely still do it.' As a fighter, that was the sort of encouragement I needed. So that was the start of a great relationship between me and Harry Holland. From the way I had been feeling, speaking to Harry gave me back the faith in myself that had disappeared, and I decided that I would carry on boxing. But I promised myself that, if any other British fighter beat me after 'Bomber', I would definitely bloody quit.

As soon as I started working with Harry, one of the first things he told me was that I should move up to super-middleweight, which was something I didn't want to do at first, to be honest. I was quite confident and comfortable at middleweight. But Harry said, 'No, James, we will go up, because all these guys who have been boxing at middleweight are jumping up to super-middle.' I have to say that it proved to be a smart move by Harry to bring me up to super-middleweight because that was the division where I would get more opportunities. It showed good judgement from Harry as a manager and, as a fighter, that was all that I was looking for, a manager to really guide me or even say something to me to make me believe that it was possible. All I wanted was just that chance to prove myself, and I ended up getting that chance thanks to Harry Holland.

Harry's gym was over in Greenford, and it used to take me bloody two hours to get there and two hours to get back, and that was if I was lucky. It was probably a bit quicker coming back, but the traffic on the way over there used to be horrible. But I thought, 'This is where my manager is and this is where his fighters are, so this is where I need to be.' I used to go running in the mornings, go to work, and then at five o'clock I would make my way over to Harry's gym to start training at seven o'clock in the evening. So, by the time I got home again at night, it was a long day.

Brian Lawrence had come back to train me now that I had left Darkie, so that was a very good thing. Also, there was another trainer in the gym called Johnny Bloomfield, who was Harry's right-hand man. So, in my corner for my fights, it would be Brian Lawrence, Johnny Bloomfield and Harry, and it worked out all right. If Brian wasn't there at the gym for whatever reason, Johnny would take over and train me a little bit. If I wanted a bit of pad work or something like that, Johnny used to help me out and get me sparring with the other boys in the gym. Johnny Bloomfield was a big guy and he was a nice guy, and we all had a lot of respect for him. You never really saw Johnny raise his voice or anything like that. There were times when Harry would get a bit upset and have a go at the boys, but Johnny was always a cool guy. Johnny was like the master of keeping everybody happy and quiet, and he was a lovely man.

It was at Harry's gym where I met Ali Forbes for the first time. Ali was a very good fighter who ended up winning the

British super-middleweight title. Ali was a Brockley boy and I had a cousin living in Brockley who Ali knew well, so Ali and me ended up becoming good friends, and we still are today. If you met Ali, you would probably think that he was a very smooth talker, but the man was so tough and sparring with him helped me a great deal. Ali was so rugged and he would come at you non-stop all the time, so you had to work hard when he was there in front of you. I would never be happy getting ready for a fight if Ali wasn't in the gym for me to spar with.

The thing with Harry was that he used to call everybody 'mucker'. Harry would always be saying, 'All right, mucker? How are you doing, mucker?' Me and Ali Forbes had never heard that word before, and we used to sit together in the changing room discussing it between us. 'What is all this mucker business? What the fuck is this word, mucker? What does it mean? What is he calling us? How come nobody else uses this word except Harry?' Sometimes, me and Ali used to sit in the back of Harry's car and we used to take the mickey out of him, saying 'All right, mucker? How're you doing, mucker?'

Another one of Harry's boys who I used to spar with regular was Andy Till, who they used to call 'Stone Face'. Andy was such a tough man, and he still is today. He was a proper old-school fighter, and he went on to win the Lonsdale Belt outright at light-middleweight. I was sparring with Andy one time and I was really working on my right uppercut. As Andy came forward, I hit him with an uppercut and it took the front of his blasted nose right off! There was blood everywhere.

Brian Lawrence immediately shouted, 'Stop!' and Andy says, 'It's too fucking late for that!' So Andy took himself straight off to the hospital to get stitched up, and then he came back and he *still* wanted to spar. He put on a full-face headguard that covered his nose, and he was saying, 'Come on! Let's go again.' That is the way Andy was.

Sometimes, after training, we used to hang around for a bit and talk to each other about our lives. We would talk about what job we did, and stuff like that. Andy Till was a milkman. In fact, his other ring name was 'The Mental Milkman'. Andy said to me one time, 'James, this morning while I was out on my milk round, there was a young kid who took a pint of milk off my float.' So I said to him, 'Andy, what did you do?' He said, 'I chased him, I caught him and I took back the fucking milk.' Andy was that type of guy.

The man they called The Explosive Rocky Kelly was another great character who was at Harry's gym at the same time as me. Rocky was Southern Area welterweight champion, and he was such a ferocious fighter with a massive following of fans who really loved him. We had Serg Fame, who was Southern Area light-heavyweight champion. Robert Smith, who is now the secretary of the British Boxing Board of Control, used to come over to the gym for sparring quite a lot. So we had a great bunch of guys at Harry's place, and the atmosphere was brilliant.

My first fight after I signed with Harry was scheduled to be an eight-rounder with Errol Christie on 31 January 1989. Errol came from Coventry, but he lived in south London and he was another Brockley boy who also trained at Harry's gym. Errol would be there with his manager, Burt McCarthy, and his trainer, Les Southey. One day, me and Errol had a sparring session. Before we got in there, Harry told me to hold back on the power a bit. Harry said, 'James, don't show too much because this could be a fight in the making.' So Errol looked good in the sparring session and, the next week, Harry says to me, 'Right, you are fighting Errol Christie.'

When you think about it, after losing to Herol Graham, Errol Christie was a very good fight for me to come back with because, at that point in time, Errol Christie was by far the bigger name out of the pair of us and I knew that a lot of people were looking at me as the underdog. In reality, I think it was a 50/50 fight, in the sense that whoever lost was going downhill.

Errol had been such an outstanding amateur. He was like this golden boy, and I felt like he'd had everything given to him in the boxing world. By the time he fought me, he had a few losses on his record and I believe he knew that he had to beat me in order to stay in the bigger picture. As for me, I was feeling that, because I had been beat by Herol Graham in my last fight, if I didn't beat Errol Christie, I wasn't going nowhere and I might as well jack it in. If I were to lose to Errol Christie at that stage in my career, with the losses abroad and everything else, the only fights that I would probably have managed to get after that were the type of jobs where you are just being used as a name to go in with younger fighters who were considered hot prospects, and I definitely didn't want to be going down that road.

The fight took place at York Hall, and the place was absolutely packed out. I would say that we had equal support on the night because we were both Londoners, so it was like, 'Who is going to be the man of the town, Christie from Brockley or Cook from Peckham? I think that was probably the most tickets I ever sold although, in actual fact, I probably only sold about ten tickets. I gave away the rest.

The bell went and I put Errol down in the first round, and he looked shocked. He got up at the count of two, he sort of sat back down, and then he got up again at the count of nine. It was a good and exciting fight, and we had the crowd on their feet all the way through. In the end, I stopped him in five. The referee was Richie Davies, and he moved in to put an end to the fight when I had Errol sort of slumping against the ropes.

Like many of my former opponents, Errol became a good friend to me. When you have the type of fight that we had, you form a bond with each other that comes from mutual respect. Me and Errol always had that feeling for each other. We were mates and we loved each other right up until the end of his life, which came far too soon. Errol died of cancer on 11 June 2017 and he was only 54 years old. I went to see him two days before he passed away and, as I walked into his room at the hospice, he told one of the ladies who was looking after him, 'This is the man who bashed me up,' and he was still smiling.

It was another eight months before I was back out boxing again, and one of the fighters I was sparring with quite a lot in the meantime was Crawford Ashley, a 6ft 4in Rastafarian from Leeds, who eventually went on to become British,

Commonwealth and European light-heavyweight champion. Me and Crawford used to spar down the Henry Cooper gym in the Old Kent Road, and he was such a hard man to bloody hit. When you were in the ring with Crawford, you had to be switched on all the time because boxing-wise he had such a great brain. Crawford was very awkward to spar with and he used to be a thinker, so that meant that you had to think how to set up an attack. To be honest, I couldn't stay with Crawford boxing-wise at long range, so I used to try and get to him as quick as possible at close range so as not to give him time to think. One of the things about sparring with Crawford that was great was that it gave me plenty of rounds in the ring with a man who was taller than me, which was something that I wasn't used to. It was just as well because my next opponent was practically the same bloody size as Crawford.

In September 1989, I took part in a final eliminator for the British super-middleweight title against Brian Schumacher, who came from Liverpool. We boxed at Latchmere Baths in Battersea, and I have to say that Brian Schumacher was the tallest guy I ever fought. Even though I had recently put in plenty of rounds sparring with Crawford, to actually *fight* someone taller than me was different. As a fighter, I always wanted to have the height over somebody, so that, when you get to the weigh-in, you can stand up there and you will be looking down at your opponent. When we were at the weigh-in, Brian Lawrence says to me, 'Have you ever fought anybody taller than you before?' I said, 'No.' So he said, 'Well, you are now!'

It meant everything to me to have another chance to fight for the British title and I really didn't want to let the opportunity get away, so I had it in my head that I would just get close to Brian Schumacher and get him out of there quick. I think that was the only time that I ever climbed through the ropes with that mentality in my mind, because I still felt a bit bad about the Herol 'Bomber' Graham fight, when I didn't feel that I did myself justice. When it came to boxing Brian Schumacher, I wanted to make sure that I got it right. So I decided that I wasn't going to box him or take my time with him the way I usually did. I wanted to go out there and fight. I wanted to put him under pressure and I wanted to stop him. I stopped him in the fifth round and, to be quite honest, it happened quicker than I expected.

I was elated about winning that fight, and I was on a bit of a high for a few days afterwards. I had stopped Errol Christie in five. Then I stopped Brian Schumacher in five. I was starting to think that five must be my lucky number and I was beginning to feel unbeatable. But unfortunately, you can't beat someone if there is nobody standing in front of you to beat, and I never got a sniff of another fight for over a year after that. I don't know why, but there were just no opportunities out there for me. So I just had to carry on training and wait for my chance to fight for the British title.

In October 1990, after all the eliminators and final eliminators that I had been involved in, I finally got my shot at the British super-middleweight title. I was matched up to challenge the champion, Sam Storey, who was a tough

Irishman. Storey had only lost once previously in 16 fights and that was to Steve Collins. He had fought most of his fights in Ulster, and he was a real local hero over there. Harry had wanted to get me the home advantage and put the fight on with his Winners Worldwide promotion company in London, but it didn't happen that way and we had to travel.

For me, the thought of going to Belfast was frightening. All I knew about it was what I used to see on the news, soldiers with guns and people throwing burning bottles. We flew over to Ireland in one of those small aeroplanes, and I was a little bit nervous because I could sort of feel the engine shaking. We got off the plane and into a cab, and the driver said, 'Where are you staying?' So we gave him the address and he told us that we would be staying at the most regularly bombed hotel in Belfast. When the cabbie told us that, we couldn't *believe* it! We were laughing, but it wasn't a happy laugh. It was a nervous laugh.

We arrived at the hotel and we made our way to the weigh-in, and there were soldiers with guns and tanks everywhere. While we were driving by, it felt like they were pointing their guns full on us. Before that day, the only guns I had ever seen in my whole life were the little toy guns that I used to buy myself when I was a kid and the guns that you see on the bloody TV. This was the first time I had ever seen a *real* gun. There were so many of them, and to see those guns being pointed in your direction was very scary. The Irish boxing promoter, Barney Eastwood, was in the car with us and, when we came to a certain checkpoint, they could see that we were with Barney and you could kind of *feel* them take their hands off the triggers in a sense. It was a frightening experience, and I must admit that I was seriously starting to think about the fact that I had left my family back in London. I found myself hoping that I would get back home to them again after it was all over.

That night, which was obviously the night before the fight, the staff at the hotel woke all the guests up at about midnight and they got us all out of the hotel. They told us that we had to be evacuated because there had been a threat about a Semtex bomb being somewhere inside the hotel. But I must admit that the staff sorted the whole thing out pretty quickly, and it wasn't long before they had confirmed that it was safe and then they let us back into the hotel. The sad thing was that things like bomb scares were happening so often over there that those lovely people who were looking after our safety that night had become used to the situation, so they just took it all in their stride.

Me and Sam Storey boxed at the Maysfield Leisure Centre in Belfast and, as you can imagine, it was packed out with his Irish fans. When I went in for that fight, in my mind, there was just no way that I was going to get beat. I thought I would bide my time, and then destroy him with an uppercut. The referee was Mickey Vann, and he stopped the fight without a count when I caught Sam Storey for the second time with my right uppercut in the tenth round. I had finally become British champion, and obviously I felt unbelievably happy and tremendously proud when they wrapped the Lonsdale Belt around my waist. But I didn't celebrate the way that I wanted to directly after the fight was stopped, and that was because I was frightened.

The troubles were still ragging in Belfast and, for a Londoner to come over there and win the British title, me being a black guy as well, I had it in my mind that the crowd might boil over. But, to be honest, I can only say great things about the Irish fans. Where I had thought that they might get angry and upset because I had come over there and stopped Sammy Storey, it wasn't anything like that at all. The Irish absolutely love their sport, and the crowd that night were a knowledgeable crowd about boxing. Whereas I had been frightened when I had first arrived in Belfast, in the end, I felt better walking about over there than I did in bloody Sheffield! When I was coming home, people at the airport were saying to me, 'Cor, we saw you on the TV. That was a great fight!' Those Irish people really enjoyed watching me box and I must have come home with about three bottles of whiskey, and I don't even bloody drink whiskey!

In March 1991, Harry secured me the opportunity to challenge for the vacant European super-middleweight title. In the other corner would be a man named Pierre-Frank Winterstein, who was a rugged, shady character known as the 'King of the French Gypsies', and it turned out that I was going to have to travel to Paris to fight him. I was originally supposed to be up against his stablemate, but the opponent got switched at the last minute and they brought Winterstein in instead. When he fought me, Winterstein had a record of

50 wins in 52 fights, 37 by knockout, and I knew that he was a world-rated fighter. But, after the wins against Christie, Schumacher and Storey, I felt confident and strong, not to mention the fact that I was getting paid £30,000 for the fight, which was my biggest purse yet and more money than I had ever seen in my whole life.

When we arrived in Paris, we stayed together in our tight little group. My corner had an addition with us that night, a trainer called Lenny Gregory, who used to train a welterweight from Islington called Daren Dyer at Harry's gym. Lenny Gregory was one of these hard trainers who wouldn't take no crap from anybody. Sometimes, if Brian Lawrence or Johnny Bloomfield weren't in the gym, Lenny used to help me out on the pads and things. So I decided to pay for him to come over to France and be in my corner because that was my way of saying thank you to him and, to be honest, I was very glad that he was there. There was just a weird feeling about the atmosphere surrounding that whole fight, and I was happy to have as many good men out there with me as possible.

It turned out that Pierre-Frank Winterstein's people had a lot to do with the promotion and, when we arrived at the weigh-in, everybody seemed to be speaking French. To be honest, it sounded like they were going on about a whole heap of nonsense, but we didn't have a clue what they were saying. Luckily for us, Simon Block was out there on behalf of the British Boxing Board of Control, and I have to say that Simon was an angel that night. It turned out that Simon could speak French and, all of a sudden, Simon just switched and started to speak French. Simon turned around and he said quietly in my ear, 'Don't worry, James, I've got this in hand.' Sure enough, once Winterstein's mob realised that Simon was there and he understood what they had been saying, people were suddenly speaking English. After the weigh-in, we went off to get something to eat. I had been warned by somebody not to eat the food in the hotel where we were staying, so I went for a walk around the corner and I found a nice little café. I'm not quite sure who it was, but somebody who was with us ate the food at the hotel and he had the runs all night.

One of the other British boxers who was fighting another Frenchman on the same show was the Southern Area lightweight champion at the time, a fella called Ian Honeywood. Ian is such a funny guy and, on the plane on the way over there, he was cracking jokes non-stop. I really love Ian Honeywood, but he is also a madman because he could have got us *killed* at the press conference. We were sitting on one side of the table and the French boxers were sitting on the other, and Ian kept nudging me and pointing over at Pierre-Frank Winterstein and saying, 'James, look at the size of his nose. You can't *miss* his nose!' I was saying, 'Shut up! They can bloody hear us! They can understand English!'

Me and Pierre-Frank Winterstein boxed in a big convention centre in the middle of Paris, and I think his supporters thought that they were as tough as the man they had come to see. They certainly made enough noise anyway. It turned out to be a very hard fight, with us both standing toe to toe a lot of the time. He knocked me down in round nine, but I wouldn't say that I was badly dazed by it. It happened at the end of the round, and I remember getting up and walking back to my corner. I don't know if I was saved by the bell, but Winterstein's corner were going mad and blaming the referee for not stopping the fight. I felt fine coming out for the tenth, and I have to say I boxed brilliant in that round. I just showed him that I wasn't hurt and I wasn't going to run, and I think I just broke his heart from there. In the end, I stopped him in the 12th round with my right uppercut.

It was a bad knockout. When Winterstein went down, he hit the canvas face first and he didn't move. He stayed on the floor for quite a while and, believe me, it is a horrible feeling when you put a man down and he doesn't get up more or less straightaway. In a situation like that, a minute can seem like an hour. All the time that Winterstein stayed on the floor, we were worried for him, but we were also worried for ourselves as well. If we were in the same situation in London, we would be sure that we were going to get out of the venue in one piece. But, when you go abroad, you are never quite sure what to expect. A year earlier, Derek Williams had gone to France to defend his European heavyweight title, and I remembered hearing that the crowd had been chucking chairs at him. This was the same sort of crowd. The air was tense and we were expecting bad things to happen.

We got out of the ring and walked back to the changing room without anybody saying anything or doing anything to us, and then I had to give a urine test for drugs. After going almost the full 12 rounds with Winterstein, I was pretty drained, so I was drinking loads of water, having cold showers, marching up and down and jumping around, just so that I could do a wee-wee so that the doctor could take it for the blasted test. I knew that they definitely wouldn't be letting me go until I had managed it because they were following me everywhere I went. In the end, God knows how, but I was able to provide them with their sample and they went away and left me alone.

Suddenly, this bloke appeared in the changing room and he came marching straight over to me. He had all these men standing around him, and he said to me, 'Cook, can we have your shorts?' I'd had a nice pair of black shorts made especially for that fight. This was the first time that I had ever had shorts made the way that I wanted, with my name on and things. So I said, 'No, you can't have these shorts because I only just had them made. But I've got a spare pair in my bag and I will sign them for you if you like.' But the fella shook his head and he said, 'No, Cook, what I mean is I want *those* shorts,' and he pointed to the ones I was wearing. That was when I heard a spooky whisper in my ear, 'Cook, this man is the *real* king of the French gypsies. Just give him the shorts.' So I whipped off my new shorts as quick as a flash, and I signed them and handed them over.

For me, becoming the European champion was like being a world champion. I was 31 years old and, although I hadn't originally planned to still be boxing at that age, things were just beginning to go good for me now, so I decided to stick around for a few more years and see what might happen. For some reason, and I can't remember why, before I could defend my European belt, they told me that I had to relinquish my British title. I wasn't jumping for joy about it, but all sorts of things go on behind the scenes in boxing. By this stage, I had learned to just go with the flow and do the best thing for my own career, and I knew that the European title obviously held more weight than the British.

Three months after becoming European super-middleweight champion, I was scheduled to defend my title against my old sparring partner Mark Kaylor, which was good thinking by Harry Holland because, although Kaylor was past his best by this stage, he was still a big name who could draw a big crowd. When me and Mark Kaylor were matched to box each other, it was billed as two gentlemen having a cup of tea. There was no other way they could have billed the fight between me and Kaylor, because we never slagged each other off. Everybody knew that he used to pay me to be his sparring partner and I think some of the press reporters tried to make a bit of a thing about that, but me and Mark just got on with publicising the fight and there was no bad-mouthing between us.

When the TV cameras came to film us at the weigh-in, they had us sitting next to each other both drinking tea out of a cup and saucer. I suppose we must have looked like chalk and cheese, in the sense that Mark was this clean-cut guy wearing a smart suit with a shirt and tie, and then there was me with my afro hairstyle and my big moustache. I used to tell people that the afro hair used to help me keep my balance because I was so skinny. But, in all seriousness, it was just a hairstyle at the time that I liked. The moustache never got cut all the way through my career, because that was sort of my trademark and they used to call me 'The Bandit'. The moustache was me making a statement, saying, 'I am not going to shave this off until I finish boxing.' I used to let Carmen trim it up for me sometimes, but that was it.

Even though I knew Mark Kaylor personally, I never had that feeling about fighting him that I did with Mick Courtney or Dudley McKenzie. By this time, he was 30 years old and I was 32. I had a far greater understanding of the boxing business than I did in those early years, and I also knew that Mark wanted to beat me. Mark was a cool guy and he never said anything in front of the cameras and the microphones, but I knew that, deep down, he must have been coming to fight me thinking to himself, 'Hang on, I used to pay this guy to spar with me.' But this fight was for *my* European title, and the boot was on the other foot now. I was thinking, 'Listen, maybe you used to pay me to spar with you, but this is *me* giving you a shot at *my* title now.' That was a great feeling for me.

We boxed at York Hall on a boiling hot June evening, and the place was packed with Kaylor's fans. Because I was the reigning champion, Mark came out to the ring first, and his music was always the West Ham football song, 'I'm Forever Blowing Bubbles'. When it was my turn to come out, my ring-walk song was 'U Can't Touch This' by MC Hammer. When they announced Kaylor's name, his fans went mad. When they called out my name, it seemed like the whole place was booing.

It was like I was a stranger. I knew that York Hall would be full of Kaylor's supporters but, when they introduced us, I thought, 'Oh, my God!' But I always tried to block out these things and just concentrate on the person in front of me, so I just concentrated on Mark.

I knew only too well how rough he was and I knew that he was a very hard man. I knew that you had to practically *kill* Mark Kaylor to stop him coming forward, and I had prepared so well for him that, no matter what he brought to the fight that night, there was no way that he was going to see 12 rounds. I was expecting him to pressure me because he couldn't box me, in the sense that I was the better boxer, so I trained for the pressure, and that was just as well because he never stopped trying to get to me in the whole fight. Kaylor was such a natural fighter and I liked people who came on to me wanting to have a fight, because people didn't expect me to be so versatile with my movement. I was long and lanky, but I could chuck really good short punches.

I could feel that I was starting to get warmed up on Kaylor from the beginning of the sixth round, and it's hard to explain if you have never boxed, but I just knew that it was simply a matter of time. Whether he was going to be stopped because of a cut or a knockout or whatever, something was going to happen, because I was starting to punch at will now. I was really rocking him.

I got to him with the right uppercut in the end, and it happened just before the end of the sixth. Mark's legs went a bit slack and he sort of lay back on the ropes. His eyes were sort of glazed and, as I went in after him, Mark's trainer, Jimmy Tibbs, threw in the towel. Mickey Vann was the referee and he was facing the wrong way to see the towel. I saw the towel come flying in and land on the canvas somewhere behind Mickey's back, so I kind of eased off on the power. But, because Mark was facing me and he also had his back to Jimmy, he didn't see the towel coming in either and he was still throwing shots at me with both hands. He was still so willing to fight because that was the type of man that Mark was, so I thought I had better fight back a bit, just in case he went and bloody caught me.

The next thing I knew, I saw Jimmy Tibbs had actually climbed into the ring and suddenly he was in amongst us, and that was when Mickey Vann stopped the fight. You see, Mark was in front of me and his legs were going, and it is at times like that when a man can get seriously hurt, so Jimmy did a great job that night. It was one of the best things that I have ever seen a trainer do and, at the time, a lot of people didn't give Jimmy Tibbs enough credit for that. I would say that it was a beautiful stoppage at the right moment.

So far as Mickey Vann is concerned, I have to say that I thought he was a brilliant referee. Mickey was up on his toes all the time. He used to move around that ring like he was a dancer, backwards and forwards, and somehow he always seemed to be within touching distance. But, at the same time, he was never in the way and he would let you get on with the job. To be fair to Mickey, I think it was a lot more unusual for the towel to be thrown in back then and, like I said, he wasn't in the right position to see the towel when Jimmy threw it in to the ring.

As for Mark Kaylor, he was one of the bravest men in boxing. Kaylor would be on the floor, and he would *still* want to get at you. When he first realised the fight had been stopped, he wasn't happy about it at all, but he calmed down again quickly because him and Jimmy were very, very close and Mark knew that Jimmy had only done it for the best of reasons. After it was all over, I walked over to Mark. I told him that it had been a good fight. I took hold of his fist and I raised it in the air, and then I gave him a little kiss.

As soon as they realised what was happening and the fight was finished, the crowd started to get a bit ugly. A few of Kaylor's fans did kick off. There was a little bit of fighting and things going on around the ringside after the fight, and all I could do was stay in the ring and look out into the crowd for Carmen and all my supporters. I just wanted to make sure that they were okay. But the security guys got to the action pretty quick and they did an expert job of calming it all down.

A lot of people used to say that Mark Kaylor's fans were racist because they were West Ham football fans. I would say that they were definitely *aggressive*, but West Ham fans would normally want to fight anybody anyway. I suppose you could say that Kaylor's fans were the most hostile fans I ever boxed in front of. I mean, even though I had boxed in France in front of a crowd of French gypsies and I had marched out to fight Herol 'Bomber' Graham in front of his fans in Sheffield, the difference was that the Kaylor crowd actually started to fight amongst each other. But I don't know if they were particularly racist. Anyway, I used to put all of that out of my head when I was in the ring. To me, supporters were just supporters.

In my honest opinion, if I had fought Mark Kaylor earlier in his career when he was the Kaylor of old, when he was the Kaylor who beat Roy Gumbs, I reckon that he would definitely have beat me because, in those days, he had this man strength that I simply didn't have. So it all came together for me at the right time, and Mark retired for good after fighting me.

After the Kaylor fight, I think there was about six months left on my contract with Harry Holland. I honestly never thought that this would happen to me, but I had people whispering in my ears telling me that I should go to Mickey Duff, because Mickey was the biggest promoter out there at the time. The thing was, at that stage of the game, I really wanted to be having regular fights. Whereas Harry Holland might put on a show every three months or every six months, Mickey Duff was putting on shows nearly every week. All I can say is that one thing led to another and, in the end, Harry did the right thing. He got on the phone to Mickey and he told him, 'Jimmy Cook wants to come over to you.' Harry and Mickey made a deal that paid Harry out for the rest of my contract, and then I was free to go.

I want to say here and now that I will always be grateful to Harry Holland because it was Harry who had faith in me at the time when I really needed it. It was Harry who made me believe in myself again after the loss to Herol 'Bomber' Graham. It was Harry who put me back on track and in the position to fight for and win the British and European titles. So I have got to give Harry Holland all the credit in the world. Without him, I wouldn't have been in the position to go to Mickey Duff. Harry was good to me back then and I will never forget that. I still see Harry about, he still calls me 'mucker', and I am happy to say that we are still good friends to this day.

MICKEY DUFF

FROM the moment I signed up with Mickey Duff, we got along with each other very well. Mickey Duff kind of liked me and the people in his office liked me, so I never had no problems with Mickey. He made it very clear to me from the start that he believed in my ability to challenge for a world title and win a world title, and I believed that he was the man to be with if I was going to get the opportunities that I needed. Mickey Duff was a very, very clever man who knew his boxing inside-out and, after all the ups and downs that I had experienced throughout my professional career, I just wanted somebody to look after me and guide me.

Believe it or not, I didn't know nothing about the damn taxman until I walked into Mickey's office. One of the first things he asked me was, 'Have you got yourself an accountant?' I said, 'What do you mean, an accountant?' Mickey tried to hide it, but I could see that he was really shocked when I asked him that question. He fixed me up to see an accountant straightaway and I honestly believe that, if it wasn't for Mickey Duff sorting my life out, I probably would have gone to prison.

It turned out that I owed about £18,000 in tax. Mickey spoke to the tax office at the Elephant & Castle on my behalf and he arranged it so that I had to pay back £50 a week.

Sometimes, I don't think that fighters always realise that the promoters have got to declare to the taxman who they have paid out money to. Some fighters don't understand that they need to keep on top of these things and they need to make the situation work for them. As soon as Mickey had set me up with that accountant, I was claiming for my boots, I was claiming for my socks, I was claiming for my bandages and anything else that I bought. Mickey Duff taught me that, once you get yourself a good accountant, then you are good to go.

Being with Mickey was an education in many ways. For example, I didn't know anything about gambling in casinos in those days. One day, Mickey took me to this massive one on the Edgware Road and, as we walked in through the door, these big guys came towards us with their hands out. I honestly believed that they were going to rush me, so I put my fists up ready for a fight, and Mickey said, 'No, no, no, James, they are only coming to take your jacket!'

We went over to this gambling table and Mickey took £100 out of his wallet. He put on a couple of bets and he lost his money, and then he won it all back with a bit more on top. That was when he turned around to me and said, 'Come on, James, it's time to go.' I said, 'But, Mickey, you just got your money back. Don't you want to try and win some more?' But Mickey says to me, 'James, trust me, if I stay here any longer, it will all be gone.' So that was a great lesson in life.

Because of the amount of times that I had broken my right hand, one of the knuckles had completely gone and I kept having trouble with it. I had to have two operations on it, and they put a metal pin inside there to try to heal it. Up until I went with Mickey Duff, it had given me trouble throughout my career. I was having treatment and I was going to clinics, but nobody had ever sorted out the problem. Even if it stopped hurting for a little while, the pain would always come back after I'd had a fight. Mickey sent me to Harley Street and this clever doctor said to me, 'When you are taping your hands, just make sure it's level.' Something as simple as that was all it took, and I couldn't believe it. I said to Mickey, 'Who is paying the bill for that?' Mickey said, 'Don't worry, James, I will pay for it.'

Alongside Mickey Duff there was Dennie Mancini, who was a great trainer. Dennie was also a matchmaker and he had a manager's licence as well. He was a brilliant man in British boxing, and my relationship with Dennie was great. Dennie would always advise you well, he spoke to you well, and he always treated you like a human being. I learnt to wrap hands from Dennie Mancini because, when he used to wrap your hands, he used to wrap them so perfectly and you used to feel so good. Dennie was also a brilliant cuts man, and he was a wonderful guy to have in your corner. So, between Mickey Duff and Dennie Mancini, I felt that I was in a very good place.

Mickey Duff was a great businessman. He would say to me, 'James, I am not interested in what I can earn from a fighter this month. I am thinking about what I can earn from that fighter years down the line.' That was where Mickey was different to most of the other managers. Mickey was willing to take a chance with fighters if he decided that they were worth it. I got some great advice from him, and I know that he enjoyed working with me. I remember we were talking in his office one time and he said to me, 'James, why don't you ever give me any trouble? You pay me. You *must* make me work for you. Everybody else does!'

Up until I signed up with Mickey, I had always been told that I would have to sell tickets, because that is what most promoters do. They tell you that, if you can't sell tickets, you won't get any work. Selling tickets was never a big issue as far as Mickey Duff was concerned, because he already had Billy Schwer, who would sell the blasted place out on his own. Billy was a good-looking and popular guy, and he was also a great fighter who went on to win British, Commonwealth, European and IBO world titles. He was also a champion ticket-seller. So anybody selling more tickets after Billy was a bonus, which was just as well for me because most of my fans were black people and black people didn't tend to buy tickets.

I did have one young lady who followed me everywhere she could. Her name was Nicola Cartwright and I had been working with her from when she was a child, because she grew up around the estate and she used to come to the after-school club that I was running. When Nicola came to watch me boxing, her mum always used to come with her. I remember one time when I was boxing at York Hall and the pair of them were screaming their heads off. After I retired from boxing, Nicola kept my shorts and some other stuff. So at least I can say that I did have one fan. Nicola was my fan. She still lives just up the road from me, and she is married now with a couple of kids.

A month before I had my first fight for Mickey Duff, something truly terrible took place that rocked us all in the boxing world very badly. On 21 September 1991, Michael Watson had his second fight with Chris Eubank, which left Michael literally battling for his life. In the week leading up to that fight, something very disturbing happened that nobody will ever be able to explain.

Carmen was out in Tenerife on holiday with her sister and her friends. On the Friday, the day before the fight was going to take place, Carmen rang me up and she was *so* very upset. She said to me, 'James, I had a dream last night. I dreamt about Michael, and it was a really bad dream. I dreamt that Michael came to me, and he was wrapped up from the top of his head right down to his feet in bandages like a mummy.' In Carmen's dream, Michael had said to her, 'Carmen, look at what Chris has done to me.' Carmen sounded so desperate on the phone. She was saying, 'James, please call the Boxing Board and tell them to stop the fight. Please, James, do it. Please, don't let Michael fight.' I had to try and gently explain to Carmen that I simply could not ring up the British Boxing Board of Control and tell them to stop a world title fight because Carmen has had a dream. I had to get it across to her that the Board of Control would have told me that I was crazy. They would have said, 'What is *wrong* with you?' They would be telling people, 'Jimmy Cook has gone *mad*!' Whenever I think back to that phone call, it still makes my blood run cold.

I was not at White Hart Lane on the night of the fight, so I stayed at home and I watched it on the telly. In the 11th round, when Michael put Chris down, and then Chris got up and put Michael down just before the bell, I couldn't believe what I was seeing. When Michael came out of his corner for the 12th round, when you look back with hindsight, it was obvious that his legs were still weak and he hadn't fully recovered from the knockdown. But the situation and the mood had become so heated in that arena and everybody was so caught up in the excitement.

Then, after Chris stopped Michael at the beginning of the 12th round, they showed you Michael's corner briefly and it looked like he was starting to collapse. A few minutes later, they showed Michael down on the floor and, when I didn't see Michael get back up and lots of people were running around, I knew that the situation was deadly serious. Usually, when a fighter goes down like that, after a few minutes they put the fighter on his stool and you know he is all right. I sat there watching the TV screen and my heart felt so heavy. It was probably in the early hours of the morning when somebody rang me and told me that Michael was in a bad way and they had taken him to hospital. But I still didn't really know just how badly Michael was hurt and, although he had gone to hospital, I was still hoping that he was going to be okay because he was in the hospital. I thought that he was in the best place and I honestly believed that he would be fine.

When that happened to Michael, everybody in the world was rushing down to see him. I didn't go to the hospital or anything because there were so many people going, and I was thinking, 'Okay, he is going to need somebody to be around after you guys have gone.' I think a lot of it was all about the fact that it was on the news and things, and some people wanted to be connected with the situation because of that little bit of excitement. So I waited for a little bit until a lot of these people had disappeared, and that was when I made my approach. The first time that I went to see Michael in hospital, it was very hard because I was looking at this fit, strong man who I had boxed and it was difficult to stand there and see how badly he was struggling.

Me and Michael are still great friends to this day, and we are even tighter now than we were before. Michael is like my son now and, every now and then, I have to sort of slap him to keep him in check! The other day, he said to me, 'Jimmy, it was a blessing that you beat me, papa,' and I said, 'That is right, because you were a bit too flash!' As you get older, you realise that some things happen for a reason. Because of that happening to Michael, the British Boxing Board of Control is probably the safest boxing authority in the world for looking after fighters. Before that happened to Michael, they never had all these safety measures that they have got in place now, with the hospitals being on alert and the medical staff being at ringside. It is indeed a terrible thing that Michael was the one who had to pay the price, but the main thing is that he is still here with us all today. We are speaking, we are laughing, we are telling jokes and, believe me, Michael is pretty sharp when he wants to be.

The first fight that Mickey Duff arranged for me was a defence of my European title against Tarmo Uusivirta in October 1991. We boxed at Latchmere Leisure Centre and, after I went to Finland and done ten rounds with Tarmo in a bloody ice rink only to get robbed of the decision as I saw it, there was no way on this earth that I was going to let him beat me again. This was my title on the line, plus it was also a final eliminator for the WBA world title, so it was very important to me.

At the weigh-in, Tarmo was trying to make out that he wasn't scared, but I knew that he *was* scared. His brother was with him and he was trying to be in my face, saying to me, 'You're not good enough. Who have you fought?' But I just ignored the brother, and I turned around to Tarmo and I said, 'Well, I fought *you*, didn't I? I might have lost to you on points over in Finland, but there is a big difference now. You are fighting me in *my* town now, so let's see what happens.'

As soon as the fight began, I was very determined that I would get to him early on. It was a fight where, every time I hit him, I hurt him. I have to say that, when Tarmo retired in the seventh round, it was sweet revenge for me and, after the problems with the money when I fought him in Finland, it felt good to stop him. I have to say that it was a strange surrender, because he just sort of turned his back on me during the fight. But, in boxing terms, it was probably one of the best revenge fights for me. I was still European champion, I was a step closer to boxing for a world title, and the only way I could see things going was in an upward direction.

The thing about this life is that we never know what is going to happen next, and sometimes I think that is just as well. In my next fight, I went out to France to make another defence of my European title against a guy named Frank Nicotra, and he bloody stopped me in the first damn round.

Frank Nicotra's girlfriend was with him at the weigh-in, and she was so scared that she was almost in tears, and I thought that Nicotra himself was looking pretty nervous. But, by now, experience had taught me that, when a man is nervous, he is also dangerous. Also the thing that I hadn't told anybody was, the night before that fight, my brother and Carmen had phoned me to tell me that my mum was in hospital, and I don't think I hardly slept at all that night. All I wanted to do was just get on with the fight, go out there and hit him, and then come back home to see mum. She had been taken to Maudsley Hospital, which was for people who have had a nervous breakdown. When we were growing up, we used to tease each other and say, 'Your mum and dad are in Maudsley Hospital.' We used to call it the mad hospital, but that was when we were just little kids. When I found out that my mum was in there, I was so worried and I just wanted to get home to her.

So, when it came to the fight with Frank Nicotra, I thought to myself, 'Okay, let me go out and hit him on the chin and get home.' But *he* hit *me* instead! He got in there first and he chucked the first punch, and I walked straight on to that punch. So my plan backfired. *I* was the one who got hit and *he* was the one who went off to a party!

Steve Holdsworth was commentating on that fight for Eurosport, and Steve said on the telly that he was going to put his house down on me. He said, 'There ain't no *way* this French guy is going to beat Jimmy Cook. This boy, Nicotra, is not in Cook's class. I would bet my house on that.' Anyway, the way things worked out, I am so damn glad that Steve never put his house down on me beating Frank Nicotra, because these things happen in boxing and Steve might have ended up sleeping outside on the street if he had.

After losing my European title, I became very depressed. I felt sort of disappointed by Mickey Duff, because I'd had to defend my title against Frank Nicotra in France. He was six years younger than me and he was unbeaten in 27 fights. I would have thought that Mickey could have found an easier defence for me than that, and I felt devastated because a world title shot had now gone out of the window. But, there again, there are usually two sides to every story and I have to say that the money that I got paid was very good. It was £60,000, which was the biggest payday I ever had.

My sister, Angela, was getting married and one of my first jobs when I got back after I lost my European title was to give her away at her wedding. I wasn't marked up for the wedding or anything like that, because the thing was it was just one shot that finished the fight. To be honest, to look at me, you wouldn't have thought that I had even *been* in a fight. But the best thing and the most important thing was that Maudsley Hospital made my mum better again. I thank that hospital so much, because they sorted mum out and gave her medication, and then mum was mum again, which was brilliant. That was more important than anything.

Mickey told me that he planned to get me back in line to fight for the British title, but I just couldn't seem to find the motivation that I had in the past and the edge went off my training. I was coming in late and I wasn't resting properly. I couldn't believe that I had to go and prove myself again at the age of 33. I had been working at this boxing game for nearly 20 years, and I had never taken any shortcuts with my training. I would go out there and run miles. I would punch the bags. I would spar. I had been doing all of this for so long, and I felt tired. But I also knew that, despite the way that I was feeling, I still needed to have some more fights to secure the future for my family. So I fought on for a further two and a half years after that and I had another eight fights before I finally finished.

Five months after the loss to Nicotra, I was matched to box Tony Booth, a journeyman from Hull who was a very tough customer. Tony Booth was a proper character. If you happened to be in a clinch with him on the ropes, he might lean over and start talking to the people at ringside and he was full of tricks like that. But, even though he liked to play the clown, Tony Booth was nobody's fool. In those days, Tony was up in Sheffield with Brendan Ingle and he was much cleverer than a lot of people thought. Tony was very slippery, and you couldn't hit him for too long because he didn't stand there for you to hit him, and I could tell that he was fresh that night. We boxed at York Hall in September 1992, and I beat him on points over eight rounds, but it was a hard slog because I knew that, if I started slacking in any way, Tony could have beat me.

A month later, I boxed Terry Magee. He was a former Irish champion, and he had shared the ring with many good fighters and beaten quite a few of them. But, by the time I boxed Terry Magee, he was heading towards the end of his career and he was getting beat on a regular basis. We boxed at Wembley Arena on the same night that Frank Bruno stopped Pierre Coetzer in eight rounds. My fight with Magee was on straight after Frank's fight and, because I used to like to fight off the ropes a lot, the first thing I used to do when I climbed into a boxing ring was test the ropes. So, that night, I was bouncing about testing all the ropes and I nearly fell out of the blasted ring, because bloody Frank Bruno and Pierre Coetzer had broken one of the damn ropes! Anyway, they changed the rope and I stopped Terry Magee in the fifth round.

In January the following year, I boxed an eight-rounder with a man from Birmingham named Carlos Christie, who was like another journeyman really. Just like Terry Magee, Carlos Christie had shared the ring with the best. In fact, almost four years to the day after he fought me, Carlos Christie ended up having his last fight with none other than Joe Calzaghe, and he went out on his shield when Calzaghe stopped him in two.

We boxed at the Elephant & Castle in January 1993 and, to be honest, back in the days when I was firing on all cylinders, Carlos Christie was the type of man who I really should have stopped. I *did* go out there to try and stop him, but the best that I could do was to beat him on points. It is difficult to explain, but it was like something in my body wouldn't operate the way that I wanted it to operate. I couldn't get that flurry going when I was putting my punches together, and I knew for definite after that fight that I either needed a rest from boxing or I was getting too old to be a fighter.

Six weeks later, I boxed Karl Barwise of Tooting, another journeyman who, believe it or not, also had his career ended a few years later at the hands of Joe Calzaghe. We boxed at Lewisham Theatre, and I felt a little bit more fired up that night, so I stopped him in the sixth round.

Mickey Duff was true to his word, and he secured me another shot at the British super-middleweight title, which was vacant at the time. I boxed a man named Fidel Castro Smith, another fighter who came from Brendan Ingle's gym. Apparently, Brendan Ingle used to give some of his fighters funny Irish names and he used to call Fidel Castro Smith 'Slugger O'Toole'. Anyway, I didn't know any of this and I had never seen a picture of Smith, so I just pictured him as being an Irishman. So the first time that I laid eyes on Fidel Castro Smith, I was shocked to see another black man.

I felt so tired during that fight. Mickey Duff was going mad with me in the corner. Everything Mickey could have shouted and told me, he told me that night. Fidel Castro Smith shouldn't have been a hard fight for me at that stage. I took the title on points. But, if you want me to be honest, that was the only fight that I actually think I lost, fair and square. I think I needed a favour that night and, for once, the decision went my way.

The referee was John Coyle and, even in the moments when he was actually raising my hand to declare that I was once again British champion, I was actually very upset with myself. I might have got the decision, but I didn't feel that I had won the fight as clean as I wanted to. In the years that had passed by, I had been going through rounds and I would feel stronger as the fight went on. That night, I didn't feel strong. I didn't have none of that pumped-up feeling that I used to have and I knew that my fighting spirit wasn't the same. So I wasn't comfortable with the win, which was a strange feeling. Even though I had just regained the British title, I felt kind of deflated. One thing I knew for certain was that I definitely didn't want to carry on boxing for too much longer. What I really wanted was a defence of my title to make as much money as I could, and then come out of boxing. I was now 34 years old and enough was enough.

Six weeks later, I was supposed to be boxing a man named 'J.J.' Cooke, a light-heavyweight from Coventry, but he pulled out at the last minute for some reason. I was supposed to be getting £10,000 for the fight and, when Mickey Duff rang me up to tell me that my opponent had pulled out, he asked me how much I expected him to pay me. When I told him that I was expecting to be paid £10,000, fight or no fight, Mickey just laughed and he said, 'You want £10,000 for *not* boxing? Don't you worry, James. For ten grand, I will definitely have somebody there for you to fight, no problem.' In the end, good old Tony Booth stepped in and saved the day, so me and Tony ended up fighting each other a second time.

When Tony Booth and Brendan Ingle turned up at the weigh-in, Tony jumped on the scales and then he jumped back off again pretty quick. Before we knew it, Tony was dressed and the pair of them were off out of the door. All of this made Mickey Duff very suspicious, so Mickey went chasing after them into the car park, but they were too fast for Mickey. By the time he got out there, Tony and Brendan were driving off in Brendan's car, and they were both smiling and waving at Mickey. It turned out that Tony was at least a stone heavier than me when we stepped into the ring, but Mickey said, 'Don't worry, James, I will get him the next time.'

I won the fight against Tony on points over eight rounds, but it felt just like a workout really. I was just going through the motions and I didn't even think about trying to stop him. As far as I was concerned, it was another paid job while I was waiting for a defence of my British title, and that was all. But I mean absolutely no disrespect to Tony Booth when I say that. Let me tell you now that, when Tony Booth was on top of his game, he was a damn good fighter.

As for Brendan Ingle, I have always had nothing but respect for him because he was a small guy and he brought all these big champions through, like Prince Naseem Hamed and Herol 'Bomber' Graham. Also, Brendan was a nice person, and you have to give credit to nice people. Brendan would never show off or act like he didn't know you, which a lot of the more high-profile promoters or trainers would sometimes do. I always had a little chat and a little laugh with Brendan.

It turned out that I had two more fights left in me. The first was another eight-rounder against Karl Barwise. We boxed at the Aston Villa Leisure Centre in Birmingham and, after stopping him the first time we boxed, this time I beat him on points.

My last fight in the ring took place at York Hall on 11 March 1994. I had been telling Mickey Duff that all I wanted now was a defence of my British title and, first of all, Mickey had suggested having a rematch with Fidel Castro Smith, but there was no way I was fighting *him* again. I knew that I had been lucky against him the last time, and I still had that memory in my mind. So I said to Mickey, 'No, I'm not going to fight him again. Get me somebody else.' So Mickey looked through the ratings and he says, 'James, there ain't nobody there for you to fight, but I've got a young man here. He is white, he is 24 years old and he sells tickets.' So I asked, 'Who is it?' He said, 'His name is Cornelius Carr.' I said, 'That will do fine and don't worry, Mickey, because I am going to stop him.'

There was a man missing in my corner for the fight with Cornelius Carr, and that was my trainer, Brian Lawrence. Shortly after the Karl Barwise fight, Mickey Duff had asked Brian if he would train Henry Akinwande, a heavyweight from Dulwich, and Brian said that he would. Boxing is a hard business and every man has to look out for himself. My career was coming to an end and Henry Akinwande was Commonwealth and European champion, and he was flying high. It turned out that Henry was boxing somewhere else at the same time that I was defending my British title, and Brian made the decision to go and be with him. So sadly, the way things worked it, it turned out that Brian Lawrence wasn't in my corner for my final fight. But I understood completely that Brian had to do what he felt was right for him at that time. By now, I was a big man of 34 years old and I knew that I could do without Brian that night, so I wasn't really all that bothered.

The people who were most unhappy about it were actually my kids, because obviously, with me and Brian being together for so long and with me having made quite a name for myself, the girls had seen this man being in my corner for all these years and all they knew was that he wasn't there for the last one. They were saying that Brian shouldn't have gone off with Henry Akinwande because it was me that brought him through. But, to be honest, I would say that me and Brian both brought each other through because obviously he was my coach and, most of the time, he was there for me. Sometimes, if you are a coach and you are working with more than one fighter, you have to make a choice. But the girls were not seeing it that way and, to be honest, they are still a bit annoyed about it, even now. They just love their dad, and that is all there is to it.

That night in the ring with Cornelius Carr at York Hall, I think it was during the seventh round when I was looking over at him and I was thinking to myself, 'A couple of years ago, I would have knocked you out!' I was trying to trick him and set him up for some sort of big attack, but he was always a step ahead of me. I don't want to take anything away from Cornelius because he beat me on points, but I honestly don't know if he won the fight. Even though he put me down, I didn't think he won the fight. But the discipline was in me not to argue about it. Boxing has taken me all over the world, and it is not right for people to see James Cook start shouting.

Thinking about it now, I don't want to downgrade Cornelius Carr's performance because he turned up and he didn't have to take the fight. In all honesty, I was probably too overconfident. I was thinking to myself that he was only 24 years old and I would probably have too much for him or I would know too much for him, but the fact was that I said that I was going to stop him and I didn't. He was very smart. He boxed very clever, and I did try my bloody hardest to knock him out. But it never happened. So I accepted the decision peacefully and quietly, and I also accepted the fact that my boxing career was over.

I did say that, if any British fighter beat me again after Herol 'Bomber' Graham, I would retire, and that is what I did. I knew that the time had come for me to step down from the ring. Even if I hadn't retired then, I knew that Mickey Duff would probably have got me an eight-rounder somewhere and he would have kept me going. But I didn't want to become one of these fighters who overdid it, because I had boxed in an era where everybody was tough and everybody was strong.

I will never forget a conversation that I had once with Marvin Hagler. Marvin said to me, 'When you retire, don't ever come back. If you never did it then, what makes you think you're gonna do it now?' I know what Marvin meant. It gets harder as you get older. Boxing is a young man's game, and it's not like football. You don't have a team on the pitch to help you out. You don't have ten men running around who will give you a pass. When the bell goes, you are in that ring all by yourself.

A lot of fighters carry on boxing too long, but in a lot of cases it is not because they don't know when to quit. It is because they haven't earned the money that they expected to earn, so they carry on because they think they are going to earn it. I remember talking to Barry Hearn when he first came into boxing. Barry was a straightforward guy and I liked him, so I listened to what he had to say. He told me, 'James, if a fighter gets a house out of boxing, he's done something.' Nowadays, I know exactly what Barry meant, and I am pleased to say that I've got my house. So, to me, I think I've done all right, because I wasn't thinking about anything else, just getting something for my girls, and this house will be theirs one day.

I don't think a lot of people realise how hard it is to be a fighter. One of the reasons I liked Barry Hearn was that everybody on his shows got fed well and looked after properly. In some other situations, you could end up struggling for a meal. You would be struggling for food and things like that. I started off earning £150 and ended up earning £60,000, so I don't think I did too badly. But it wasn't like I had earned millions of pounds or anything like that.

Mickey Duff advised me well, as he always did. He said to me that I could do one of two things with my money. I could buy a house or I could open a business for my missus. So I gave Carmen the money and she opened a hairdressing salon and, believe me, there have been times over the years when Carmen's shop was the only thing that fed us.

I am always telling people that you should never be jealous of the next person, because you don't know what they have had to do to earn their bread and butter. Boxing is hard, and some of the guys who go on too long experience problems later in life. Also, a lot of boxers experience a lot of emotional pain when they retire from boxing. It affects a lot of them psychologically, because they feel lost after the fighting finishes and they don't know what to do with themselves. Luckily, that never happened to me. I loved my boxing career. In the end, I retired with no regrets, and I was grateful for the experience of being a professional boxer.

THE BOXING COACH

I KNEW that I needed to decide what I was going to do next, and I wanted to do something that would allow me to pass on the boxing knowledge that people had passed on to me throughout my time in the ring. So, about three months after my retirement, I made my mind up and decided to go for my professional trainer's licence. Just like the way I started off in the pro game as a fighter, in my mind, I didn't think too big as a coach either. I wasn't looking for no champions. Right from the start, it was always in my head that I would take a fighter who the world considers to be a nobody and I would train that fighter to be a somebody. I think, for you to really learn something, you have got to start off as a nobody.

If somebody had asked me to train Mike Tyson, I probably wouldn't want to do it because Mike Tyson was already a great fighter. What I would want to do would be to train somebody starting at the bottom to *beat* Mike Tyson. I think the reason I felt that way was because I was seen as an underdog when I first started out, and I went on to achieve what people never dreamt I would achieve. Maybe I felt empathy with these types of fighters because I remembered all too clearly how it felt when *I* was in that position. There were plenty of guys who were supposed to be superstars in front of me and they never made it. I *did* make it, but I knew the amount of sacrifice and hard work that I had to put in to get there. I knew that you didn't have to be a gold medallist to be a professional champion. I knew that hard work and doing the *right* work is what matters the most. If I could do it, I knew that I could teach other boxers to do it too.

Once I had applied for and received my professional trainer's licence and I was ready to go, I knew that I needed a gym to work from. This was when Ian Honeywood, the boy that nearly got us murdered in Paris by the 'King of the French Gypsies', really helped me out in a big way. Thanks to Ian, I ended up running the two famous gyms above the Thomas A'Becket and the Henry Cooper pubs, both of which were situated in the Old Kent Road. Ian Honeywood used to run a pub, so he had all the contacts and I honestly don't know how he did it, but he ended up getting me into the Thomas A'Becket first. Then he was managing the nightclub downstairs at the Henry Cooper and he said to me that he could get me in the gym upstairs, so then we shifted from the Becket down to the Cooper.

In both cases, Ian went to see the people that needed to be seen, and he sorted out either as little rent as possible or no rent at all. Now, this is two of the most famous boxing gyms in London and I ended up running them both for a while. These are great places where I grew up knowing that Muhammad Ali had trained there, Henry Cooper had trained there, Terry Downes had trained there, and all these very famous fighters. So Ian Honeywood might have nearly got us bloody buried by the French gypsies, but he certainly made up for it in the end.

We don't always appreciate the things that God gives us in this life. But, all the time I ran these special boxing gyms, I was aware that I was doing an important job, in the sense that I was ensuring that these places carried on as boxing gyms. These days, life changes so much all the time and, when I look back at some of the great places and traditions that used to be around, it is just not there anymore. These gyms were a massive part of British boxing history. These gyms were landmark places and, with all the money that is out there, I think it is a damn shame that people couldn't come together and save them. Even if they weren't being used as actual boxing gyms, if somebody with money had preserved these great places like little museums, then people would still be able to go there and see where all these legendary fighters had trained. Anyway, they are both gone now, which I think is very sad.

Once I was set up in the gym and I got going as a trainer, I found I had quite a lot of fighters coming to me more or less straightaway. I think, to be honest, people knew that I could fight and it wasn't too long before the gym was really buzzing. It would be impossible to say how many fighters have passed through my hands in one way or another since I took out my professional trainer's licence, but I would guess that it would probably be 100, at least.

The first fighter I trained was Matt Brown, a super-featherweight from Walworth. Matt has got these funky legs. Matt is like a ballet dancer. When he was younger, somebody ran over his feet in a car. So, instead of walking flat-footed, Matt would be in the ring and he would be sort of up on his toes, and he was kind of bow-legged. When Matt first came to the gym to see me, I took one look at him and I said, 'You've got funny legs.' So he looked at me and he said, 'Yeah, but nobody has got more heart than me.' Fair play to Matt because he was right. He *did* have a lot of fighting heart.

Matt Brown actually became my first champion. He won the Southern Area super-featherweight title against a Brixton kid called Marcus McCrae. They boxed in December 1996 at the Elephant & Castle. The crowd was mainly from Brixton and I wouldn't call them hostile, but them Brixton guys didn't think Matt had a chance in hell. Although Matt actually had a very good record at the time, they just thought he wouldn't have the boxing ability to beat Marcus McCrae. But, when a lot of people realised that Matt was being trained by me that night, when they saw me in his corner, I think they started to think a little differently about what the result might be. The longer the fight went on, the more Matt started to take control. In the end, Matt went out and stopped Marcus McCrae in the ninth round, and Marcus never boxed again after that.

Also, I was very proud to have Dennie Mancini in the corner with me that night as well. At first, I had been a bit shy about asking Dennie to help me out because I had always considered guys like him to be well above me. But, when I mentioned it to Dennie, he said he would be more than happy to work with me, which was great because Matt Brown used to cut easily. So I had the best cuts man in the business working with one of my fighters and I couldn't have asked for nothing better. After that, whenever I asked Dennie to come and work with me, he was right there every time.

Matt Brown challenged for the British title twice, first at super-featherweight and then at lightweight, and those were the last two fights he ever had. You see, not all that long after Matt came to me to train him, he got married and he bought a house. Matt was a grafter. So, even when he was supposed to be resting, I knew that he was probably going home and working on the house. He was a young man who was full of energy, and I knew what was happening. To be honest, I think that was probably the reason why Matt never won the British title, because I don't think he gave himself enough time to rest. But at least Matt was honest. If he hadn't done his running or something, he would tell you straight that he hadn't done it. Matt would always tell you the truth.

Another Southern Area champion I trained in the early days was Allan Gray, who won the title at middleweight. Allan was just like Matt Brown in the sense that, if he hadn't been doing his running or something like that, he would be honest and tell me. These are the sort of fighters who are easy to work with. Allan's dad was very knowledgeable about boxing and he was a very good advisor, so he also used to help out at the gym.

We made a great team, and they were very happy times. The fighters I was training were starting to win titles, and that was a great feeling for me. I had already proved myself as a fighter, and now I felt that I was proving myself as a coach.

I have always believed that one of the most important things about the relationship between a boxer and his coach is respect. If I was training a fighter and he wasn't listening to me, it would never work out. There were a pair of boxing brothers from Guyana who lived in Battersea called Gilbert and Howard Eastman, and Dennie Mancini asked me to train Howard. I think I trained Howard for about three fights and he won them all. But, one night, we were in the gym and I told him to chuck a shot, and he said that he wasn't going to do it. When I asked him why, he told me he didn't need to be practising all these shots because he was just going to knock his opponent out. So that was the end of our relationship because, no matter how good you are, everybody needs a coach to advise them. Howard was a damn good fighter. He ended up becoming British, Commonwealth and European middleweight champion. But he probably would have been a world champion if he'd listened to who was around him, whether that was me or whoever trained him afterwards.

As it happened, I also trained the other brother, Gilbert Eastman, for a while. Gilbert was a good fighter who won the Southern Area light-middleweight title. Gilbert was always ready to listen and he was always ready to train hard. He ended up challenging Gary Lockett for the WBU world middleweight title and he got knocked out in the first round. He got stopped again in his next fight and, to be honest, I encouraged him to retire from boxing after that. Then he made a comeback and he collapsed after his final fight against Sam Webb. They had to rush him to hospital and operate on him to remove a blood clot from his brain. Thank God, they managed to save him and he came through. I still hear from Gilbert from time to time, and he is doing okay. He has recovered. He is speaking. He is doing everything well, and Gilbert is a nice guy.

Boxing is such a dangerous sport, which is why it is so important for fighters to keep themselves fit and well at all times. A lot of people think that boxers are all clean-living athletes, but in reality that is not always the case. If any of my fighters were not living right, I could always tell. I used to train a welterweight from Clapham called Shabba Edwards. I will always remember one time when Shabba was matched up to box one of Dennie Mancini's unbeaten fighters, and I knew that Shabba used to drink and smoke a lot. Before that fight, I said to Shabba, 'When you leave the gym, don't fucking smoke and don't bloody drink because, if you do, I'm gonna damn well crucify you!'

So, a few days before the fight, I just happened to be driving down one of these cobbled roads up the West End and I saw somebody walking along the pavement puffing on a bloody cigarette, and I thought, 'That's Shabba!' So I drove up beside him and I says, 'Hey, Shabba, what's happening?' So he put the fucking fag behind him and, while I was talking to him, I could see the cigarette was burning something behind his back. So, as I was driving off, I leaned out of the window and I shouted, 'By the way, Shabba, you are burning up at the back.' He soon forgot to hide his blasted fag then, I can tell you! Shabba didn't have a great record, but he was all right. Dennie's fighter went all out to stop him that night, but it wasn't happening. Afterwards, Dennie said to me, 'Fucking hell, James, what have you *done* to him?'

There has always been a strong sense of competition between myself and the fighters I have trained, especially when it comes to running. When you have retired and you speak like you had a good career among young fighters with everything to prove, the competition is fierce. But all of them lot used to struggle to beat me. We used to go sprinting in the park, and they could never outsprint me or outrun me. They probably could do it now, but they couldn't have done it then.

I used to train a fighter named Spencer Fearon, who came from Forest Hill. Spencer was a good fighter, and he ended up challenging for the Southern Area title at middleweight and light-middle. I used to go out running with Spencer over London Bridge and the Elephant & Castle, and Spencer used to pass this old bloke every morning and give him some money. The first morning me and Spencer went out for a run together, the old bloke was waiting for Spencer. As Spencer ran past him, he said, 'Good morning, Spencer.' The second day, the old fella looked up at the black man running past him and he said, 'Good morning, Spencer,' and I said, 'No, I'm not Spencer. Spencer is back down there!'

I was always telling them, 'You guys are very lucky that you weren't fighting when I was around.' I would always demand the same of them that I did of myself, the same fitness, the same everything. I would let them know that I am the only one who sees them training and sparring. I am the only one who sees them running. I am closer to them than their bloody girlfriends or their wives. I would let them know when they could have a rest and when they could take a day off. The only excuses that I would take would have to come from their damn mothers. I would let them know that this is their big chance in life to do something great, and I would get very angry if I thought they were squandering that chance by not taking it seriously enough.

One of the most naturally talented boxers that I have ever trained was Ted Bami, a light-welterweight who lived in Brixton. Ted was an absolutely brilliant fighter who went on to become European and WBF world champion. But I knew that Ted had a lot of distractions because he was originally from the Congo and he was a big star in France, so he used to go over there for little holidays and he also had a barbershop. So I knew that Ted was running around a lot and he wasn't resting enough.

There was one time when we were down Finsbury Park running and Ted wasn't performing well. Me and Ted were doing ten sprints together up the hill, and I think I must have won eight or nine of them sprints. After the last one was done, Ted fell down on to his back like he was completely done in, and I went mad with him because he was so unfit. I was cursing at him and swearing, calling him a dickhead and a fool. But, when Ted went to get his medical, they told him that he had skipped a beat of his heart and he'd had a little palpitation, or something like that. Thankfully, it wasn't anything serious. The thing was I couldn't believe that I had been bloody shouting at him, but we had a laugh about it in the gym anyway.

It was actually Lloyd Honeyghan who first brought Ted down the gym because, when Ted turned professional, he signed up with Lloyd as his manager. One evening, Ted said to me, 'James, I want Lloyd to manage me and I want you to train me.' The first thing I said was, 'I have no problem with that, but make sure that you clear it with Lloyd.' Anyway, Lloyd said that he was fine with it and I started training Ted, but it wasn't long before there were bad feelings between me and Lloyd.

The problem was that Ted wasn't getting enough fights. One day, I received a phone call from Jess Harding, who was promoting shows with Barry Hearn by then. Jess said that they had a couple of fighters from abroad on this show they were putting on at the Novotel in Hammersmith, and he asked me if Ted could fight one of them. At the time, to be honest, I knew that Ted wasn't training 100 per cent, but I also knew that he needed the money. So I took the fight and Ted ended up getting beat. After the fight, Lloyd Honeyghan came over and he started swearing at me, so I chucked a punch at him and I knocked him over the barrier. I remember Barry Hearn said to me, 'Good right hand, James. Do you want to make a comeback?'

So that was pretty much the end of the relationship between me and Lloyd for the time being, but these things happen in boxing. Whatever differences there were between us back then, that was just business. Lloyd was a man who reached the top of his game in boxing, and nobody will ever forget how he caused that major bloody upset when he beat Donald Curry in America for the world welterweight title. These days, as far as Lloyd is concerned, I sort of love the man and I have nothing but respect for him and for what he achieved.

It was when we had moved to the Henry Cooper gym that I am very pleased to say that a man named Bruce Baker came into my life. Bruce was a boxing manager and a small hall promoter, and he is one of the best men that I have met in boxing. Funnily enough, the first time me and Bruce spoke to each other, we actually had an argument, or at least I wanted to have an argument with Bruce anyway.

I was training a super-featherweight from Highbury at the time named Eddie Sica, who was in the gym sparring with one of Bruce's fighters, who was a big ticket-seller. The pair had been sparring for the whole week and Bruce's fighter had been getting the better of Eddie for most of that time. But, on the last day of sparring, Eddie was the one who was coming out on top, and that was when Bruce walked into the gym. Bruce told his fighter to stop sparring, because Bruce is a protective type of guy. So I said to Bruce, 'What are you talking about? They have been sparring all week, and you weren't here when *your* boy was getting the better of it.' I was quite irate, but Bruce is a very calm guy. Bruce never said nothing nasty back to me, which was typical of Bruce. Bruce just held up his hands and he said, 'Okay, I may be wrong.'

After that, I soon realised that Bruce was a great guy and we became good friends very quick. The thing about Bruce is that he is such an honest man. In the boxing business, a lot of managers and matchmakers will tell you this and tell you that, but you never know if you can believe them or not because there are so many untruths flying about all the time. If Bruce Baker wanted one of my boxers to appear on one of his shows and my guy was unlikely to be walking away with a win, Bruce would tell me straight. He would say, 'He ain't going to win, James, but it's a good payday for him.' So I always got honesty from Bruce right from the start, and he had a good sense of humour too. If he used to come out and about with us, quite often he would be the only one with white skin and fair hair, and I used to call him 'the drug dealer'.

Bruce came to me one day and he said, 'James, will you train Delroy Mellis?' I knew that Delroy's record was not great and, at first, I said no because Delroy had lost so many fights. So Bruce said to me, 'Yeah, but all he needs is a good coach. He's tough enough. Come on, James, train him for me. You can give him something that nobody else can.' So I said to Bruce, 'Who is he going to fight?' Bruce said, 'He's fighting Wayne Alexander.' Wayne Alexander was one of the biggest punchers in Britain at the time, and I said, 'Hell, no! How long have we got?' Bruce says, 'You've got eight weeks.' But I just knew that I could do something with Delroy in that time, so I took him for the eight weeks and we did what we needed to do. Then we went down to Wales and Delroy knocked Wayne Alexander out. That was a great night for me because *nobody* had expected Delroy to do that. I was so proud of Delroy that night.

Mind you, when Delroy boxed Takaloo in Scotland a couple of years later, it was a different story. Takaloo was by far the better boxer out of them both, but Delroy had the power and he was more of a natural fighter. Delroy had Takaloo bleeding, so in the corner I was saying to Delroy, 'Right, go out there and knock him out!' But Delroy just went back out there and kept boxing away. I was thinking, 'Fuck! What is he doing?' So we were back in the corner and I was saying, 'Delroy, for *fuck's* sake, you just have to go forward and hit him for the referee to stop the fight!' So Delroy goes back out there and he was touching and moving, and this happened all the way through the fight.

In the end, Takaloo got the points decision and, when the fight was done, I was *so* upset. As soon as we walked back into the changing room, I ripped off my jacket and I said to Delroy, 'You never hit *him*, so you might as well fight *me!*' When I asked him why he never just marched out there and stopped Takaloo, it turned out that Delroy was going to Spain the next day to meet his girlfriend's mum and he didn't want to be bruised up. That *really* pissed me off.

I got home at three o'clock in the morning, and I said to Carmen, 'Where is Lisa?' By this point, Lisa was a big girl in her early twenties, and Carmen told me that Lisa was round at her boyfriend's place. The thing was I didn't like the boyfriend because I had noticed that Lisa was getting shy. She wasn't going out as often as she used to before she got together with him, and I was thinking that he was trying to control her. I've got four daughters. I am a man myself and I have been around men all my life, so I know what goes on and I didn't really like the pattern that I was seeing with Lisa and this boyfriend.

I had a rough idea of where the boyfriend lived, so I jumped in the car and drove down his road. When I saw Lisa's car outside his house, I parked my car and I rang Lisa up. I said, 'Tell your boyfriend to come out here. I need a word with him.' A couple of seconds later, Lisa phoned me back and she said, 'No, dad, we are not coming out.' I suppose that it was just as well really, because I was so angry that Delroy never hit Takaloo that I honestly had it in my mind to take it out on Lisa's boyfriend. That was the sort of mood I was in.

I have always been very passionate, both as a boxer and as a trainer. It is always a pleasure to work with classy fighters, and my old pro trainer, Brian Lawrence, was training a very, very good fighter called Ian Napa. I have to say that Ian was definitely Brian's success story, rather than mine, but I used to work with them in the gym and in the corner. Ian became British and European bantamweight champion, and I would definitely say that Ian Napa was one of the most talented fighters in this country. Napa was like Kirkland Laing. He was so gifted in what he did. When you put Ian Napa in to spar, you would say to the other people in the gym, 'Just watch how this guy rolls off the ropes. Watch his defence and his movement.' You just couldn't hit Napa. He was brilliant!

To be honest, I think that Ian Napa was a great example of somebody with special ability, but who was unlucky towards the end. He lost his British title to Jamie McDonnell in a very close fight that I believe Napa should have won. Then we went to Hartlepool for him to box Stuart Hall for the vacant British bantamweight title, and Ian got stopped in the eighth round. I didn't realise how much Ian was struggling with the weight by then. He had one more fight after that, which he lost on points, and that was it for him. Ian Napa is still well known in Hackney and we see each other often.

I have been abroad with fighters many times, and that is where my own experiences of boxing in these different countries has really paid off. I remember only too well what they used to try to do to me when I travelled away to box. So, all the way through as a coach, I have always been on the lookout to make sure that similar things wouldn't happen to any fighter I have been looking after. When you travel abroad with a fighter, it is important to try and make sure that everything is in place and they are as comfortable as possible.

I think probably the most hostile situation I have ever come across as a coach abroad was when Dennie Mancini let me take a light-heavyweight named Valery Odin over to Germany. Valery was a black guy from France who was based in Canning Town, and this was his first professional fight outside of Britain. When we arrived at the arena, they took us straight to the changing rooms and the place that they gave us was so small. It was like being locked up inside a tiny prison cell and we could just about bloody move in there.

The crowd were very hostile when we came out into the arena. I walked down to the ring in front of Valery and, when you are in a situation like that, you feel the adrenaline pumping and you have got to be so alert. You have got to keep your eyes on what is going on in front of you just in case anything stupid happens, because you never know what some of these people will do. Anyway, because Valery was walking behind me, what I didn't know was that, on the way to the ring, he had put a bloody mask on his face. As I stepped through the ropes to get into the ring, the referee came over and he said to me, 'Is he going to take that off?' I said, 'Take what off?' When I turned around to see what the referee was talking about, Valery was right behind me wearing this bloody devil mask! Valery was a tough boy, but his record wasn't great. He was boxing an unbeaten German and he lost the fight on points. When we were on our way out of the arena, that crowd were still shouting all sorts of things at us, and him wearing that mask didn't make things any damn better, but we managed to get out of there in one piece anyway.

When I am coming out with a fighter in front of a hostile crowd, I never really feel frightened for that fighter. No matter how nasty the crowd can be, at the end of the day, they've come to see a show and they have to allow the fighters to get inside the ring, and also there are security guards all around you, so you know that you are going to have some protection. I think the more worrying time is when you've got to leave the venue, because you wonder if some of these people could be waiting outside and something could happen.

I have always been the kind of coach who likes a happy changing room. I don't want my fighters sitting there in a quiet changing room, because they have already done all the quietness. When they go to bed, they will be running the fight through in their head. When they are out running, they will be thinking the fight through in their mind. So, when it comes to fight night, I don't want them to be thinking too deep about what is going to happen. So I like a changing room where everyone is joking and everyone is relaxed. Then, when the last 20 minutes comes, that is when I tell everybody to shut up and get out. That is when it is time to get serious and focus on the job.

The difference between being a fighter and being a coach is, when you are a coach, you need to have control. As a coach, I try and stay back. I try not to take the limelight. A lot of trainers do take the limelight, because they think it is about them as much, if not more, than the boxer. I am always the quietest man in the corner. This is not my time now. This is the boxer's time. They have done all the work, so you have to give them all the credit. Yes, you feel great when they win and you want to celebrate with them, but I always do my best to keep calm in there, whether they win or whether they lose.

I know how hard it is to be a fighter. I know how rough and tough it is in that ring. You may have the referee against you. You may have the judges against you. You may have the crowd against you. I know that there are times when they might be thinking, 'Shit! Can I go through with this?' So, when they win and they celebrate, I always stay back and make sure that the boxer is the one who gets all the attention. The only time that I will ever overshadow a boxer in front of the camera is if I know that he can do better and it's not being done. That is when I will probably get mad and start swearing in the corner.

I have thrown the towel in a few times over the years, and the time I will always remember was when I did it with Kevin Mitchell, a cruiserweight from Catford, who is one of the nicest guys you could ever meet. I forget where we were and who Kevin was fighting. But the one thing I do remember is that, by the time I had stepped out of the ring at the beginning of the first round, I heard the referee shouting, 'One, two' and, when I turned around to look, the other bloke was on the floor. So I thought, 'Fucking hell! This is good.' The bloke got up again, they carried on fighting and the first round finished. I stepped out of the ring for the beginning of the second round and, by the time I got down the steps, I heard the referee shouting, 'One, two' and, when I looked up, the bloke was on the floor again. The bloke got up and they carried on fighting. The third round came and, as I got to the bottom of the steps, I heard, 'One, two' and the bloke was down a third time. The bloke got up again and they carried on fighting. Before the fourth round started, I said to Kevin, 'All right, go and finish this fight now.' So I stepped down from the ring and I heard, 'One' and, when I looked up, there was Kevin on the fucking floor! Kevin was a very brave man and I could see that he was trying to get up, but I could also see that he was gone. So I threw the towel in straightaway that night.

By the rules, the trainer is not technically allowed to throw in the towel. By rights, you should go up to the referee at the end of a round if you want to stop a fight. But sometimes, if you can see that your man is not going to win and he is taking too many shots, the only thing that you can do is throw in the towel. That is an emergency situation, and you want the fight stopped right away. You know your fighter and you know when enough is enough, when he is taking unnecessary punches, so I think the referee should always respect it when a trainer throws in the towel.

It is survival of the fittest out there in that ring, and you don't build stamina overnight as a fighter. That is why people have got to give the journeyman fighters the greatest credit in the world. You've got to give them respect, because they are in and out of the ring every week, so they are building up this great stamina that you need for boxing. These guys are very skilful at surviving, and I don't think some people realise that fighting a man who has only come to survive can be a very hard thing to do. I always say to fighters, 'Just make sure that you are in shape when you are fighting these guys because, if there is any weakness, these guys will take advantage.' That is why I do everything I can in the gym to get everybody in top condition and, if they are not in top condition, I will want to know the reason why.

Mind you, although I am definitely a hard taskmaster, I think it's a good thing to have a little bit of fun in the gym as well. One of my training techniques is something that I saw an American trainer do on the telly not long after I became a coach. I tie lengths of string across the ring at all different angles. Then I get the boxers to shadowbox in the ring and duck under all the different strings, and I play reggae music for them while they are doing it to help them get that rhythm. It's such a good exercise for balance and movement. If a fighter has natural movement, I will add more strings, and everyone likes it. It is a good thing to do and a nice thing to see.

One of the fighters I used to train who loved the reggae and the ropes was a cruiserweight named Tommy Eastwood. Tommy was a friend of Melanie Lloyd, the lady who has helped me write this book, and it turned out that he needed a new trainer. So Mel rang me up and asked me if I would train him. I had a very good trainer called Marvin Stone working with me at the time. Marvin had boxed as a professional bantamweight, but we got to know each other after we had both retired and he came up and introduced himself to me one night at a boxing show. We hit it off straightaway, and we started training fighters at a gym in London Bridge.

I told Mel to bring Tommy with her to the gym on a Saturday afternoon and, when Tom jumped into the ring and started shadowboxing, me and Marvin stood back and watched him and we could see a lot of promise in Tommy. I ended up training Tom for about 18 months, and he was a very good fighter. He ended up becoming Southern Area champion, although I have to say that Tom did that with Les Southey as his trainer, the man who used to train Errol Christie.

Tommy was a big and powerful gypsy fella, and he fitted in very well with all the black fighters straightaway. He was a very rugged guy who radiated toughness, but he was never loud. In fact, Tommy used to speak in a quiet voice, but he had a wicked sense of humour and he was a great laugh in the gym. He also used to drive me mad sometimes! With Tommy's lifestyle, he was one of these boys who came and went a lot. He might be going great guns, and then he would suddenly disappear for a couple of weeks. But, when Tom stuck at it, he was great.

The thing with Tommy was that the hearing in one of his ears was not very good. He came up to the gym one time and I think he had probably been fighting in the street and he must have taken a clump in the other ear, so he was more or less completely deaf. He had Mel with him that night, and she told me that she'd had to shout at him all the way up there in the van. I was always shouting and swearing at Tom anyway and, on this particular night, I *really* had to shout at him all the time, just so that he could bloody hear me. After the training session was finished, straight after Tom and Mel walked out of the gym, one of my brothers rang me up and I started shouting down the phone at him. My brother was upset because he thought I was angry with him, and I said, 'No, it's that bloody Tommy Eastwood. He's had me shouting all night, and now I can't bloody stop!'

These days, when it comes to training fighters, I have stepped back from that aspect of my life considerably as my commitments and priorities have shifted over the years. Recently, I have been working a lot with Ted Bami, who had built up a nice little stable of fighters and a good name in the business side of boxing. But boxing can be a cruel sport in more ways than one, and Ted recently had a very bad experience.

Ted had been managing and training his nephew and, because Ted was the boy's uncle, he never took anything out of his fight purses. The problem seemed to be that, because Ted had not been taking anything off the fighter until he got a decent purse, when the time came for Ted to take his percentage, the fighter didn't like it. Obviously, in this day and age, we have social media to contend with. Apparently, the fighter said some stuff on there. I think the problem is that people simply like to believe bad things about other people and jump on the bandwagon. The way Ted saw it, he had taken the boy into his home and treated him like a son, and he couldn't believe it when he started getting threats from people who were hiding behind keyboards. To make things worse, all of Ted's other fighters left him over it as well.

The case ended up in front of the British Boxing Board of Control and Ted was found not to be in any way at fault, but it was a horrible time for Ted. I was there at the meeting with Ted and the Board actually advised the fighter to stay off social media, but the damage was already done. But, believe me, Ted Bami will be back. I have no doubt about that. Me and Ted have known each other a long time and I know that he will come back strong.

If any fighter has ever come to me and tried to argue with me about my trainer's fee of 10 per cent, I say, 'Listen, out of my 10 per cent, I have got to buy bandages. I have got to buy adrenaline. I have got to buy this. I have got to buy that. This 10 per cent don't even put petrol in my car.' So, if a coach gets something out of boxing, I think it is well deserved because, even if you might think, 'Oh, he's just sitting down there for two hours,' the fact is that he is there advising you. The fact is that he has left his home to be with you, so you have got to give your coach credit. Everybody needs a coach, no matter who you think you are, because sometimes it gets tough in there and, at the end of a brutal round, you just want to hear something or see somebody.

When I hear some of these fighters these days saying, 'I'm boxing and I need a fitness coach,' I break down in laughter. I think to myself, 'You are a fighter. You have got a coach there. Why do you need a fitness coach?' They are all getting food experts and all this sort of stuff, and everybody seems to be so worried about nutrition and conditioning. They have got different coaches for this and different coaches for that, but a lot of these coaches don't seem to be teaching their fighters about the skill of boxing, which just doesn't make sense to me. I sometimes wonder how much technique is being taught nowadays.

Boxing has certainly changed a lot since my day, and not always for the better. There is only one minute between rounds and you might have to tell your fighter many things in that tiny amount of time. It can be hard enough to get what you want to say across to a man who might have come back to his stool after a heavy knockdown or with an eye streaming with blood. But, these days, they want to play deafening rock music between the rounds on all these big shows. It has become what a lot of these so-called fans expect, but it is so distracting for the boxer, and also for the coach.

I suppose the thing to keep in mind is that life moves on and you have to keep up with the times. I used to swear at my fighters all the time between rounds, but then the TV people started dropping the microphone smack bang in the middle of the corner. That was when the British Boxing Board of Control wrote to me and told me off. They said to me, 'James, when you are in the corner and the microphone is near you, remember that this is a live show and cut down on your swearing.' But some things never change and, if you ever see me on the telly quietly whispering into a fighter's ear in the corner, the chances are that I will probably be telling him that he's a bloody wanker!

THE PEDRO YOUTH CLUB

EVER since I moved to Hackney, there has always been a place called the Pedro Youth Club just around the corner from where I live. The Pedro was first started in 1929 and it is one of the oldest surviving youth clubs in London. There have been many write-ups over the years in the local papers about how Elizabeth Taylor and Richard Burton became very involved with the club in the Sixties, and the Pedro became quite a famous place.

About 15 years ago, the local council decided to close the club down for good because it had run out of money. In those days, they used to nickname this area 'the murder mile' because so many young people were getting killed around here. I know for a fact that, when it comes to stabbings or shootings on our streets, we only hear about a small part of it on the news. What they tell us on the telly and in the papers is just the tip of the iceberg really. We are smack-bang in the middle of three giant housing estates and the Pedro was the only youth club around for miles. There was nothing else for the kids to do and nowhere else for them to go, and closing down a place like the Pedro just didn't make any sense to me at all.

The day the council were coming to close the doors of the club for good, I rushed over there and found the documents in the office. Then I went straight home and started making some phone calls. I rang up six people that day and they all agreed straightaway to help me. There was the boxing promoter, Frank Maloney, now Kellie, there was Bernard Hart, the founder of the Lonsdale sports brand and a great boxing man, and a brilliant lady called Geraldine Davies. Time moves on and these three are no longer involved, but I could never have managed without them back in the early days. I also rang Derek Williams, a former Commonwealth and European heavyweight champion, Marvin Stone, who had worked with me as a trainer, and the one and only Bruce Baker, all of whom are still very much involved with the club to this day.

The seven of us arranged to meet up sharpish and we formed a management committee. It turned out that the bank had paid out £19,000 to somebody with only one signature, when there needed to be two signatures to draw out money. We had the bank bang to rights and they ended up giving me the £19,000 back, so that was what we started off with. The first thing we did was pay off all the bills that were outstanding. Then we reopened the club, and we just had to keep it going with what we had left.

People tend to see me as the main man at the Pedro, and I understand that because I know somebody has to be that person. But the truth is that I have been surrounded by people who are angels right from the start. Over the years, there have been an army of people behind me who have given up so much of their time and energy to make the club work, and I would love to thank every single one of them, but there are just too many to mention them all. All I can say is that, for some reason, I seem to have been blessed by having good people around me, people of action rather than people who just speak words, and these are the people I need.

Derek Williams has always done a brilliant job as the chairman of the Pedro committee. Me and Derek were boxing at the same time, and I remember when the south London newspapers started to write about Derek Williams. I went down the gym one day and I said, 'Who is this Derek Williams?' Suddenly, Derek came out of the shower and he says, 'That's me.' I thought, 'Fucking hell, he's big!' I said, 'It is nice to meet you,' and me and Derek have always been friends since then.

Derek is 6ft 5in and, believe it or not, he has about four brothers who are all even bigger than him. They are all like giants. Derek is a great guy who is always smiling and joking. But, when you are in a committee meeting talking to people from the council who want to do this and want to do that and, in reality, they have no understanding of what is actually needed, Derek is a huge presence to have sitting at the head of the table and he takes his responsibilities as the club chairman very seriously.

Just as Marvin Stone became my right-hand man as a trainer, he is also firmly in my corner at the Pedro. Marvin has got a lot of knowledge and experience because he used to run his own van removal business, so one of the things that Marvin takes care of is the bank account. Marvin is the key signatory at the club and he holds the purse strings, so I can't get any cheques cashed without Marvin's signature.

Marvin is such a lovely guy. Marvin is always quiet and respectful, and he has some brilliant ideas, but he won't ring me up and say, 'James, we have to do this.' Marvin will ring me up and he will say, 'James, this is what I have seen, and maybe you should check it out.' Another quiet man with an excellent brain and a great heart is Bruce Baker. Bruce has had health problems over the years, but he has never stopped being a part of the Pedro. If we ever need any advice, if there is anything serious happening, Bruce is always there and ready to help.

Once we had taken charge of the club, one of the first people I went to see was a man called Ufu Niazia, who was the manager at the Pedro before the council shut it down. I asked Ufu to come back and help me out, which he readily agreed to do. Ufu was a schoolteacher so he knew what was what, and he put so much of himself into getting the Pedro back on its feet. You could see clearly that it meant so much to him. I will always be grateful to Ufu for all of his hard work, and he didn't get paid as he should have done because there was nothing to pay him with. Ufu ended up getting cancer, which was very sad. He is doing okay, but he's not well enough to work with us the way that he used to. He calls in to see us now and then because he still lives across the road, or sometimes I will phone him up and we will have a little chat.

Because there was no money, the Pedro had been allowed to get run down for quite a while before it closed, and it was definitely slow going when we were starting it back up. I would say that it probably took a couple of years for us to really win the trust of the local community enough for the kids to start walking through the doors in large numbers on a regular basis. There are a lot of parents out there who see you doing something, but they don't really understand what it is that you are trying to do. I have always been very much a rules man, every day of the week. I am definitely old-fashioned when it comes to what is allowed and what is not allowed. In the early days, I think both the parents and the kids probably didn't think that the Pedro was the place for them because the kids wouldn't be able to get away with whatever they wanted to do.

Gradually, we built the club back up again and, like a lot of things in life, word of mouth is very important. I think that everybody likes to feel safe, and these kids could see that the club was a place where they had good people ready to look out for them and who only had their best interests at heart. So the numbers started to get bigger and, at the moment, we probably get 100 or more young people coming through our doors every week. But the Pedro is not only there for the youth. The youngest we probably have is five years old and the oldest is around 70 years of age, so we have got all ages in there. The sign outside says 'Pedro Youth and Community Centre' because we want everybody in the local community to use it.

We are always looking for ways to get everybody mixing. We are running a sewing project to teach people how to sew, and we are also starting a project where we are going to get somebody in the club doing portraits, so you can come in and they will draw your picture. We are also running a keep fit class for the hospital, which is for people who have never even seen a gym before in their lives. The people who come to the class are very unfit, but they keep coming back and they try so hard. Everybody works together, and we always have a laugh. We have an over-fifties club where everybody comes in and they just play their dominoes and their games of pool. We have always wanted the club to be multifunctional. As far as we are concerned, it is all about getting the community to come together and teaching everybody to respect each other. The way we see it is, if the kids and the older people have nowhere where they can get together, how can they ever get to know each other, never mind respect each other?

An average night down the Pedro Youth Club when things are buzzing goes something like this. We open the doors at five o'clock, and we will have the young ones coming in to do their boxing. We've got a computer room, and we have got some kids doing a bit of maths and English downstairs. There is an area for them to play basketball and football outside. Some of them want to play table tennis, and one of their favourites is the Racing Rally arcade game in the corner. It is funny when you think about all this technology these youngsters have at their fingertips these days, and the thing they all seem to love the most is this machine that was donated to the club about 15 years ago. The game has been fixed so that the kids don't have to pay to have a race, and they all have a terrific time playing on that. There is a lady called Michelle and her kids come boxing, and she will be there in the kitchen doing sandwiches and stuff. So, on an average night down the Pedro, it's all happening. They get fed, they get looked after and they know that they are in a good place.

You can imagine how much work is involved to keep the show going and the Pedro can't afford to pay anybody, so everybody who is there is working on a voluntary basis. One person we couldn't do without is a man named Andy Everitt, who is in the club doing his stuff every single night. Andy is in charge of the registration forms and that type of thing, and he is always out on the door making sure that everybody signs in and out. Andy is a 6ft 6in white guy and, when people phone me up and say that they have been speaking to Andy, I tell them, 'You must have been speaking to my brother.' Then, when they come to the club and they see this big white guy, I say, 'Yeah, he's my brother from a different mother.'

Andy's wife, Laura, is also someone who really does a lot for the club. Whenever we hold a fundraising event at the Pedro, Laura is always on the door to greet people when they walk in and she is the one who takes all the money. Laura is a very warm and kind lady who gets on with everyone, and she is always looking for ways to help us. We badly needed a new carpet for our central room where everybody tends to congregate, and Laura managed to get her boss to donate a carpet, and it wasn't no cheap stuff either. That carpet has been down for a few years now and it's still looking good.

There is a man named Roy Thomas who has been by my side for the past 20 years, and Roy is in charge of all the stuff in the office. Roy takes care of all the paperwork and he deals with everything on the computer. Sometimes, when I can't remember the password to get into the computer, I have to ring Roy up to find out what it is. Roy is so loyal. His parents have been unwell and he hasn't been able to get to the club as often as he used to, so we just send everything over to him and Roy always sorts it out for us.

There is a man named Simon Hearn who is another one that the Pedro couldn't do without. Simon's daughter, Rhianna, has been coming to the club to do boxing training with me since she was about six years old. She's about 18 now and I am like a second dad to her. Simon is a school caretaker, so he likes to fix things. He likes to fix computers. He fixed the boxing bell. He helps me move stuff. He asked me how much I was paying for my fire extinguishers. I told him I was paying over £1,000, so Simon got the people from the school to come and do it and it cost me about £300. He also sorted out the alarm system for us, and Simon is the best man in the world when it comes to all the practical stuff.

I really love Simon, but I have to say that there was one time when he managed to scare the hell out of me. I went around to his place for dinner, and he said to me, 'James, I am feeding my snake.' At first, I didn't believe him, because the only thing I am scared of is snakes and I didn't think that anybody could have no damn snake as a pet. I was thinking that a snake *can't* be a pet. So I went inside the room, and there was a big glass tank with a damn snake inside there. Simon said to me, 'Shall I bring it out?' I said, 'Hell, no!' I said to him, 'Listen, you know I love you, but if that snake ever comes out of that tank while I am here, I'm jumping straight out the blasted window!' To be honest, I think snakes are probably the only things that will make me change from black to green. The thing is that I like fighting things, and I think a snake would be very hard to fight. If you are a dog, I feel I can fight you. But I can't see no way of controlling a snake. I am okay with spiders because you can slap a spider, but you can't slap a snake. Anyway, the blasted snake stayed in the glass box and we ended up having a good laugh over it. To be honest, when I think of the money that Simon has saved us, I have to let him off having a bloody snake in the house.

The Pedro lives hand to mouth really, and that has been the case all the way through since we started it back up. I think, for bills alone, it could cost us anything up to 30 grand a year. We don't get any money from the government, so we have to survive on donations. I didn't really believe in the big man above when I was younger, but I do believe in him now because, whenever it looks like we are in big trouble financially, somebody always seems to come along from somewhere to save the day. These days, I always say that, who God blesses, no man can curse.

One day not so long ago, I was sitting on my own in the club and worrying about how we were going to pay the bloody electricity bill or something like that. Suddenly, this bloke named Daniel Joseph walked in through the doors. He told me that he lived up the road and he just happened to be passing by, so he had come in to ask us what we were doing. I took him around and showed him the place, and he donated £5,000 to the club on the spot! I can't tell you how much of a weight off my mind that was. Daniel is part of the Pedro family now, and he came to the last boxing show to give out a trophy.

Sometimes, if I am stuck and I need £1,000, I will phone up Mo Prior, who is a hard-working boxing promoter, and Mo will give it to me without question. Mo is a great guy and, trust me, there have been many times when I have needed £1,000 to help sort out the bills and I've phoned up Mo. Another bunch of guys I won't forget are a team from a charity called Centrus. One time, when the Pedro was really down on its luck, Derek Williams introduced me to these guys and they really went out of their way to make sure that the Pedro survived for a year or two. So that was what saved us during that period of time.

A couple of years ago, things were looking bleak for the club and John Wischhusen, the head man at Matchroom Boxing, rang me up to say that the Matchroom Foundation was going to donate some money. So we set it up to take a few of the kids from the Pedro to a boxing show at York Hall to receive a giant cardboard cheque for £5,000 that Eddie Hearn presented to us in the ring. That five grand was a sort of lifesaver for the club. It just came out of the blue, and it couldn't have come at a better time.

The biggest single one-off donation by an individual that the club has ever received was back in 2006 from a young man named Ben Way, who I am going to talk more about later. Ben put £20,000 into the Pedro and we used that money to build a recording studio down in the basement, but there are certain conditions for the kids who want to use it. They know that they can only make what we call 'clean music' down there, and nothing else.

You see, so much of the music that the kids are making these days and putting on the internet is called 'drill music', where they are bragging about carrying knives and guns, where they are cursing each other and cursing their neighbours. They are saying stuff like, 'I live next door and I could beat you.' So, when these kids actually see each other out on the street, they want to fight each other, and it is all over nothing.

Clean music is about making a love song. It is all about making something clean. You don't need to be using language like 'bitch' or 'whore'. When I hear the young people calling each other 'nigger' and they do it in such a casual way, I think that, back in the Seventies and Eighties, we would have been fighting people for using that word against us. So we are getting the kids to sing clean music, and they can cut it and produce it, and the young people can hang on to that, which is great because, at this moment in time, clean music is what this world needs.

Down in the recording studio, I have put a list of words up on the wall that they are not allowed use. Whenever the young people go down there for the first time and they look at my list, they are shocked because these are the words they use all the time out on the street, but they can't use those words in the Pedro. When I tell them to sing me a love song, they sing

'One Love', and then they stop because they're stuck! I tell them, 'When you can sing me a love song, you can come back and use the studio.'

The thing is you have to be honest with young people because, if you are not honest with them from day one, that is when you are going to get problems. The problem is that, in this age that we are living in now, too many adults are afraid to tell young people the truth. A lot of people are too busy trying to be nice and make friends with the young people because they are scared that, if they say anything like, 'You can't do that because it is wrong,' they will end up being reported to somebody. So young people don't *expect* you to tell them the truth anymore. Whenever they are around me, I just tell them straight. As long as you put it in their heads at the start how far they can go, and give them the boundaries they need, that is when young people start to feel safe.

We started the Pedro Amateur Boxing Club about ten years ago. We had a big do to celebrate it opening, and Bob Williams came over to be the MC. Bob is the chairman of the Home Counties Ex Boxers Association. He was a good lightweight boxer back in the Nineties, and he is also an A-Star professional boxing referee, so he is a busy guy. Bob did such a good job on the day, and he also brought a load of boxing memorabilia that he auctioned to raise money for the club. The gym was absolutely rammed for the opening ceremony, and it gave everyone a good laugh when I was carried out of the ring at the end of the festivities by Derek Williams and former British and Commonwealth heavyweight champion,

Julius Francis, who is always coming down here from Norwich to show support for the club.

Since it opened, the Pedro Boxing Club has become very successful. The gym is not all that big and we have usually got about 20 boxers in there on any one night, so there is always a good and hard-working atmosphere in the place. But the one thing that seems to surprise a lot of people when they come to the boxing club for the first time is the fact that our head coach is a lady. Natasha Patterson has been our official boxing coach for quite a few years. Tash has done the boxing coaching course, level one and level two, and she is also our safeguarding officer as well as our first aider. Tash is here at the gym five nights a week, not only taking the boxing sessions but running keep fit classes as well, and she does all this for us without being paid a penny.

Tash has turned out to be an excellent coach. She watches closely all the time, and she is such a quick learner. I have to admit that these days when I go inside the gym and I watch her, I actually think she's getting better than me! Tash always wants to be a perfectionist, even with the little ones who are just feeling their way. I watch her watching them, and she's telling them, 'No, you have got to do this, you have got to do that.' Tash wants them to do it correct from day one. She's great at taking the fighters on the pads, even the big heavyweights. I say to them, 'Don't hit Tash,' but she holds her own very well. I think Tash was the only girl out of five brothers, so she *had* to hold her own. I think that Tash was probably the mad one out of them all.

I think it is sad that, in this day and age, a lot of men still don't recognise women as being equal. But, trust me, when these guys with doubtful faces walk into the gym and Tash puts them through their paces for the first time, they have to change their opinion pretty damn quick. Aside from all of the excellent work that she does in the gym, Tash also helps me run the place. When I am not there, I know that Tash is there. Tash is there with me all the time, and she is a role model. She knows her stuff, and I am so glad that she is with us. If anybody has got anything to say about the fact that she is a woman, I just tell them to go fry ice, and I instruct Tash to do the same.

The matchmaker and secretary at the boxing club is none other than Shabba Edwards, the fighter I used to train who loved smoking his fags, and Shabba does a brilliant job. He lives in south London, and he drives over to be here two nights a week. To be a good matchmaker, you need to be able to keep a lot of knowledge in your head and you have to get to know people and speak to people all the time, and Shabba is always on the phone looking for bouts for our boxers. He tells me that, when I started training him back in the day, I gave him some belief in what he was doing, and now he is here by my side. He has become a great friend, and we could never run the boxing club without Shabba in a million years.

We put on our Pedro summer boxing shows outside in the yard once a year, and the last one was show number seven. Most years, we have been kind of lucky with the weather, although there was one time when we had to cancel the boxing halfway through the first bout because it was pouring with rain. We had the singer, Junior, in the ring singing 'Mama Used to Say' before the boxing was due to begin, and then the heavens opened. But, apart from that one time, the weather has been kind to us. Last year, my two grandsons, Keiyon and Jayden, did a special dance routine in the ring before the boxing started, and the sun certainly came out for them.

Carmen and her sister, Sonia, and their friend, Babs, are in charge of the food that gets sold on the day of the boxing show. Every year, on the night before, the three of them will sit up and work right through until the morning, cleaning all this food to get it prepared for the next day. These girls are food experts and they are very particular about the way they like things done. They like to make a start on the job the night before to make sure that the food is fresh on the day. They work so hard, and the food always goes down very well.

Carmen's brother, Selvin, takes care of the music at the show every year. Between the bouts and after the show is over, he plays great songs on a top-quality sound system, and it really makes the atmosphere into something special. Carmen's other brother, Carlton, is the man who does the jerk chicken on the stall outside, and another member of my family I must mention is Carlton's daughter, Shernise, who is 15 years old. When people ring me up on the phone and I ask Shernise to answer it because I am busy, Shernise will say, 'Hello, this is James's helper.' After our boxing show last year, I just chucked everything in the room downstairs and I didn't touch it for weeks until Shernise went down there and sorted it all out. So

I suppose you could definitely say that the boxing shows are a bit of a family affair.

Steve Holdsworth, the Eurosport commentator who said he would put his house on me beating Frank Nicotra, always comes over to be the MC at the boxing shows, and he puts so much energy into it. Steve Holdsworth is like the boxing Bible. He has got such a good memory for names and faces, and he introduces all the former fighters in the crowd. Steve is a brilliant all-rounder and boxing really needs people like him. So, to this day, I am still very glad that he never actually bet his house on me beating Nicotra and, by all accounts, so is Steve!

I have to say that Steve Holdsworth has plenty of faces to introduce, because so many fighters come out every year to support the boxing show. Ian Napa regularly turns up and Prince Rodney always comes along, and Derek Williams and Marvin Stone are obviously there. Former British and Commonwealth welterweight champion Sylvester Mittee is always floating about, and also loads of the guys from the London Ex Boxers Association can be seen in the crowd, and I am going to say more about them in the next chapter.

Jason Matthews, another local boy from Hackney, always makes an appearance at the show. The first time I ever met Jason was when I was European champion and Jason's trainers brought him down the Wellington gym. Jason was still an amateur at the time. He was ABA champion and an England rep, and he was a big puncher with a ferocious fighting style. He was always knocking people out and, when I walked into the gym, Jason said that he wanted to spar with me. Jason thought that he was going to knock me out, so I gave him a beating. He rushed home afterwards and I reckon he must have gone crying to his mum, because his mum said to him, 'What is wrong with you?' He said, 'Mum, I have been sparring with the European super-middleweight champion and I didn't know.' Jason went on to become WBO world middleweight champion as a pro, and I am pleased to say that we have been friends for many, many years.

My great friend, Colin McMillan, is another regular at the show. Colin even turned up one year on crutches because he had a broken bloody foot. Me and Colin have known each other since my Lisa was in primary school. I will never forget the time when Lisa came home from school and she said, 'Dad, the school is having a special day and they want to know if you could come.' I was only Southern Area champion at the time and I wasn't sure that I would be famous enough for them, so I rang up Colin McMillan because Colin was world featherweight champion. Colin just said, 'Of course, James, no problem,' and he went up to Lisa's school to show the kids his world title belt. Lisa was so happy, and I don't think you could expect more from any friend than that.

Allan Gray, the middleweight I used to train in the early days, is always a regular at the boxing show. Allan has got his own plumbing company and, when we told him that we were starting the boxing club at the Pedro, he came over and put all the showers in for us and stuff like that. Allan did all of that for us, and he never charged us a penny.

Another great supporter of the Pedro boxing show is the referee Richie Davies. Last year, Richie and his lovely lady, Shelley, had just come back from California the day before the show, and Richie was so brown. I said to him, 'Man, you're even darker than me. When you come through immigration, you will have to tell them that you live in Peckham. Otherwise, they might not let you back into the country!' Richie has retired now, but he is another man I always respected as a great referee. When I found out that he was going to be the referee for my fight against Errol Christie, I was quite happy about that because Richie is straight down the line and he's a reasonable guy. The thing I liked about Richie is he would just let you get on with it without interfering too much and, with the Errol Christie stoppage, he did a great job.

Francis Ampofo, the former British and Commonwealth flyweight champion, who they used to call 'The Pocket Battleship', makes the journey all the way down from bloody Norwich just to support us, and I never thought I would be in a position to ring up Steve Bunce off the telly and say, 'Listen, Steve, I am having a boxing show. Please would you come?' Steve is such a pleasant and modest man when you meet him personally. Steve doesn't go putting himself about all over the place. He just stands there quietly chatting away to the boxers and the fans, and it is great to have him there.

I am delighted to say that another big personality who always turns up and makes everybody happy is John Conteh. When I think back to how shy I used to be around John in the days of the Wellington gym, when he was world light-heavyweight champion and I was just starting out as a professional fighter, it is a pleasure and an honour to say that I can phone John up and he speaks to me like an equal. John is a natural superstar, and he always has a smile and a kind word for everybody.

Another one who is always at the boxing show to help out with the fighters is Maurice Hope. Since the days of the Wellington gym, Maurice and I have become the best of friends. These days, Maurice is the national coach of the amateur squad in Antigua and, if one of his boxers happens to be over here during the time when the boxing show is on, we will always try and get the lad a bout. Maurice lives just up the road from me, and we like to sit down together and talk about boxing whenever we get the chance. I like to tease him about the Eddie Smith fight that he made with Billy Wynter all those years ago. I tell him, 'You call yourself a mate. You tried to get me bloody *beat*!' But Maurice is a cool guy, and he always just smiles and says, 'Did I?'

Because of all the hard work that Tash and Shabba put in and the popularity of the summer shows, the Pedro Boxing Club has become that well-known now that some people don't even realise it is actually part of a youth club when they go there for the first time. But the Pedro Youth Club will always come first in my eyes.

I get young kids of about five years old coming in here. They see plenty of signs on the wall about respect, manners and attitude and, at the end of the day, that is all you need, those three simple things. But young people forget them every day. They say, 'You can't shout at me.' This is the whole idea in their head. By the time some of these kids are five years old, they already think that you can't shout at them. When they go to school, they know that their teacher can't shout at them and they can't touch them.

When these kids walk through the doors of the Pedro, I say to them, 'Listen, I am not your teacher. I do things differently. You can come in here, but you either follow *my* rules or you don't come back.' To be honest, most of them listen to me, and the ones who don't listen get dragged straight back out to their parents, so they soon get to learn that I won't stand for no rubbish. Every time they come in here, I ask them, 'How was school?' They usually say, 'School was good.' So I ask them, 'Why was it good?' and they will tell me that they got a badge or a smiley face from the teacher for doing something well, and that is what I want to hear. By the time they reach ten years old, if you haven't put that respect for their elders into them by then, it is going to be far too late.

I just feel that, as a society, we seem to have lost our way a little bit and we need to get control of it. The government are making rules about what you can say to kids and what you can't say to kids, but the government aren't coming home with these people who are struggling to control their kids. A lot of these youngsters have been raised in one-parent families where there is no man figure to look up to, so they don't have respect. That is why it is so important that you have youth clubs around where somebody in there can teach these young people the right way to live.

That is why I want to keep the Pedro Club pure. I like to do things in the old-school way, and I am determined to keep the Pedro running along those lines. Young people just want somewhere where they can go and relax. They want to be somewhere where they can relate to each other and speak to sensible people. When some of these kids grow to trust you and they let their guard down when they are around you, that is when you can find out what is really going on in their lives, and then, if necessary, you can make the next move.

Most of these youths will always put up a tough front and the problem is that it is easy to think that what we see them acting like on the outside goes all the way through. Because of the peer pressure from the gang they might be hanging around with, even if they don't want to do it, they think they have got to act like this big, bad person. They don't feel like they can say no. But, when you get them away from that way of living, once you remove that pack instinct, that is when you find out that there is a softer side to their nature. I truly believe that, deep down, a lot of these youngsters *do* want to show respect, but they just haven't been taught *how* to show respect and still keep their street credibility.

There is no use in building a nice posh place for the kids where they have to take off their damn shoes to go in there. They don't want to be somewhere where they have got to wash their hands with gel before they touch anything. They don't want anybody ticking boxes and controlling and watching everything they do, because these are the sort of young people who like somewhere where they can come in and just be themselves. Over the years, we have had many visits from the local council, who want to come into the club and change things in return for better facilities, but we have always resisted that because there are always so many rules attached, and it seems to me that they aren't the rules of the real world and they certainly aren't the rules that apply around here.

Because I have always stuck to my guns in this respect, the Pedro gets no financial help from the council and the building hasn't been done up in a long time. We just do our best to keep on top of any jobs that come up along the way. So it was great when I met up again with Ray Hole, our old competition secretary from the East Lane Boxing Club who used to draw pictures of us all in the gym. These days, Ray has got his own architect firm and he is now on the Pedro Club management committee. He has drawn up some plans and he has got planning permission from Hackney Council to refurbish the club, and now he is helping us to apply for the finances we need through the right channels. I always joke with Ray and I tell him, 'It is about time you did *something* for me, because you got me some really hard fights when I was boxing in the amateurs!'

If there is any colour or creed left out of the Pedro Club, as far as I am concerned, there is a problem. When I take the kids to play football over Hackney Marshes and I look at the ethnic mix, it is really beautiful to see all these different colours and cultures blending in together. At the end of the day, they are just kids and all they want to do is enjoy themselves. Sometimes, when I am out there watching them having fun, it takes me back to the days of my own youth playing football with my pals on the North Peckham Estate.

I went to the council and told them that I wanted to start a football team, and they told me that there was already one in the area. So Roy Thomas, the man who deals with our paperwork, sent off for all the stuff that we needed and we started a team of our own, and now we have got four football teams. Our under-12s team have just won the league, and they had to beat some good estate teams, like Broadwater Farm. So we just received our first award for football, and now we want the Pedro football teams to go further.

When I first became involved with the Pedro, my main thing was to be out on the street, using the skills I had learned as an outreach worker for the Rathbone Foundation to encourage as many kids as possible to come into the club. These days, we have got so many young people to look after inside the club, so that is where I am every day, and I don't get as much time as I used to have to prowl around the estate looking for trouble. But I still like to get out there whenever I can and, when the young people pass me by, I am still shouting at them and asking them what they are doing.

Some of the young men who hang around outside the club can still remember when they were small and I would always be on their case, telling them to put their fags out and not to swear. I turned 60 years old this year, and sometimes these big lads look at me now as if they think I'm getting on. I reckon they are just waiting for me to get old. But I still like to get hold of them and pretend to rough them up or squeeze their hands tight, and I have got to say that they all have so much respect for me, and also for Carmen.

There are so many young people passing by carrying knives nowadays and, when I go outside the club and I see them walking towards me, I can tell when they are carrying a weapon just by looking at them. I have been doing this for so many years now that I can tell if a lad is carrying something that he shouldn't be carrying just by the way he moves, by the way he walks, by the way he carries himself and the look on his face, like he has got something to hide. There have been many times when I have taken a knife away from somebody, but I am happy to say that I have never had to take a gun away from anybody yet, and I thank God for that because that is something that I don't ever want to have to do.

When the drug dealers who operate around the estate drive by the Pedro in their big, flashy cars and I happen to be standing on the steps outside, they slow right down. They wind down their windows and they make a point of staring straight at me, giving me the evil eye. They know about me and they know what I do, but I have never felt under any threat from them. I have seen far too many things and I have been through far too much in my life to be intimidated by people like that. So, if they have got a problem with me being against crime and doing everything I can to prevent criminal things happening on the streets where me and my family live, as far as I am concerned, that is their problem and not mine.

Everything that happens to us along the way makes us the people we become. Without all the experiences I went through during my boxing career, the times when things got tough and fights didn't go my way, coping with people who were trying to poison my damn food, without going through all of that, I don't know if I would have had it in me to stay at the Pedro and fight battle after battle to keep it all going.

To be honest, we are still fighting those battles every day and there have been some hard times when I have found myself wondering what I am actually doing it for. There have been times when I have thought how much easier it would be to simply throw in the towel, to just stay at home and enjoy a quiet life with my family. But, in reality, I could never, ever do that because this is still the only youth club between three housing estates. I always say, 'One club, one free state.'

I am proud to say that the Pedro Club has become the heart and soul of the local community. The beautiful thing is that I could leave the doors of the club open and the people in the area would probably look after it without even thinking about it. In 30 years' time, I am going to be 90 and, if the Pedro Club is still around then, I will be a happy man. As long as there is still something good in the area for the people who live in it, then I will know that I have done what I was put on this earth to do. In the meantime, hopefully, one day soon, the gangsters in this area will realise that Hackney is not the right place for them.

THE LONDON EX-BOXERS ASSOCIATION

IT is a strange thing indeed but, ever since Melanie Lloyd wrote about me in her first *Sweet Fighting Man* book, a lot of great things have started happening in my life. It was Mel who kept telling me about how the London Ex Boxers Association was such a fantastic place and she kept saying that I must go there. They call it LEBA for short and I had obviously read all about it in *Boxing News* but, to be honest, it had never really occurred to me to go and check it out for myself. But I kept hearing such great things about the place from Mel, about how all these old fighters get together on the first Sunday morning of every month, that I decided I should go along to one of their meetings and have a look at what it was all about.

That was at least 15 years ago, and all I can say is that joining LEBA was one of the best things that I have ever done. If somebody had told me back then that this great organisation would end up becoming such an important part of my life for many years to come, I would never have believed them in a million years. In those days, the meetings were held in a big college in Stepney Green, and I don't know why, but I felt butterflies in my stomach as I was getting ready to make my way over there on that first Sunday morning. When I arrived at the college and I had parked my car, I had to phone Mel from outside the venue because, believe it or not, I was so shy that Mel had to actually come all the way downstairs and fetch me.

We went upstairs to where the meeting was being held and Mel led me into this massive room, and there were probably about 150 old boxers in there, all of them sitting or standing and quietly listening to the committee who were speaking from the front. Somebody must have passed the word down that I was there because, to my horror, the next thing I knew, they were calling my name out and asking me to get up on the stage and speak to everybody.

I can go into schools and speak to a whole classroom full of kids, no problem. I go into schools three times a week and teach the kids about boxing and keep fit, and I mentor them about knife crime and gang culture. But I have never been comfortable speaking in front of so many adults, and I was especially shy about addressing all of those guys. As I was making my way down to the front of the room, my heart was pounding and all I could think was, 'How are these people going to accept me?' I had never expected such a fine welcome in my wildest dreams and I obviously didn't have anything planned to say beforehand, but I managed to mumble a few words, and they all listened politely and gave me a nice round of applause as I made my way back to the safety of Mel and her friends.

As soon as the meeting was over at midday, the bar opened and everybody started to mingle. I was really shocked when I realised how many of these guys knew who I was and remembered my career. It was just such a great feeling for me because, growing up as a youth, I was probably watching a lot of these guys fighting on the telly and for them to accept me the way that they did was fantastic. I soon forgot to be nervous, and I started to relax and enjoy myself.

One of the first men to come over and speak to me was Bob Paget, who was Crawford Ashley's old trainer. I hadn't bumped into Bob in quite a while and it was so lovely to see his smiling face again. Back in my boxing days, it used to be quite funny because Bob was often the only white man in the gym and we used to tease him about it, although Bob never gave a damn because that is what Bob was like. Bob was a tough guy and he wasn't afraid to tell you straight. The first thing that Bob said to me that day was, 'It's nice to see you, James, but take a look around you, son. The boot is on the other foot now!' That made us both laugh because Bob was right. I think I was the only bloody black face in the room.

I honestly don't know why that was, and it is a situation that has certainly changed over the years. A few months after my first visit to LEBA, Mel persuaded Sylvester Mittee to come along as well. Sylvester was a terrific fighter who came from Saint Lucia and he boxed at the same time as me. He has always lived around my manor and we used to see each other about now and then. But, once we had both become members of LEBA, we started to see each other regular.

In fact, me and Mel and Sylvester have experienced many adventures out and about since we have all been hanging around together. Over the years, there have been new associations for ex-boxers starting up and getting stronger all the time. They operate on the same principle as the London version. They do a lot of good things for a lot of people, and me, Mel and Sylvester have been to visit them many, many times.

There was one time when we were going to Hertfordshire to attend the Home Counties Ex Boxers Association summer BBQ in my car and I had a new sat-nav, which not all that many people had at the time. Mel and Sylvester thought it was ever so posh. As we were leaving London to get on to the M25, the sat-nav says, 'This route is ambiguous.' Mel couldn't believe it. She asked me, 'Did that thing just say the word "ambiguous"?' So I said, 'Yeah, and it said it the other day as well. What does it mean?' Mel explained what it meant, and she said she was very impressed that it spoke so well.

Anyway, about 30 minutes later, we were driving round the M25 towards London Colney and I was telling them the story of how I beat up two wheel-clampers in a car park a couple of weeks earlier, which I will come back to later. The thing was, we were all so interested in the damn story that we came off the blasted M25 by accident, and suddenly found ourselves in the countryside. It was like a film. Sylvester was saying, 'Hang on. Where are we?' We were surrounded by all these green trees and the road had got very narrow. I said to Mel, 'What shall I do, get back on to the M25 or follow the sat-nav?' Mel reckoned that, if it knew how to say the word 'ambiguous', it would probably be able to find the pub. To be honest, we weren't really all that confident that it *would* find the pub because we were still doubtful about its strange magic. But we had time on our side, so we decided to give it a go and see where it ended up taking us. We drove through all these lovely country lanes and, yes, the sat-nav did indeed find the pub in the end and we had a beautiful day in the sun.

Another black brother who happened to turn up at LEBA not long after Sylvester and I arrived on the scene was Prince Rodney, and it was so great to see him there. Prince sort of came and went for a while, but these days he is a regular member who always receives a warm welcome when he walks in through the doors. We regularly see Maurice Hope, Vernon Sollas and Ricky Porter, to name just a few. Even Dennis Andries has been known to show his face once in a while, and Dennis is a man you don't see about all that often.

These days, the monthly meetings are held in a massive pub in Old Street called The William Blake. Everybody who has an interest in boxing is welcome and there are some brilliant boxing fans who turn up every month, but the membership is made up mainly of former fighters. The meeting begins at about 11 o'clock and Charlie Wright, the chairman, gets up and speaks, and then the president of the organisation, Stephen Powell, will give a little talk. After that, Ray Caulfield, the secretary, fills us in on what is happening.

The meetings last for about an hour and the guys are usually pretty well behaved all the way through, although sometimes the bell has to be rung from the stage and Charlie Wright, who is a Scouser, will get a bit stern and he'll say, 'Quiet, please!' There is often lively banter between Charlie and two other guys from Liverpool who attend the meetings regular, former heavyweight contender, Billy Aird, and his light-heavyweight mate, Pat Thompson. Those three always have the whole room laughing. They are much more funny than most of these comedians that you see on the telly.

I would say that LEBA is a brotherhood and everybody is treated the same. Champions and challengers are all as one, because the boxing fraternity is like that. One of my favourites is an old boxing booth fighter called Mickey Hayes, who had thousands of fights on the booths back in the day. Mickey is always walking around taking photographs. The following month, he will turn up with all the prints and hand them out to everybody, and Mickey will never take a damn penny for doing it. Mickey is also a great man for doing magic, whether it is card tricks or tricks with pieces of string, or whatever. Mickey can keep us all entertained for ages. He is so clever, and he is such a nice guy. He is well into his eighties now, and he turns up to LEBA every month all suited up and looking very smart.

The thing about LEBA is that you never know who you are going to bump into from one month to the next. You never know who is going to walk through the door. You might get two old boys who haven't seen each other since they shared a ring 40 or 50 years ago and, because of the fantastic network of people in that room, you get to witness these two old soldiers being reunited and they are both overjoyed, because fighters are like that. We might be prepared to punch the hell out of each other between the ropes, but we have all got nothing but total respect for each other and we often carry fond memories in our hearts of the men we have fought.

My old stablemates at Harry Holland's gym, Andy Till and Rocky Kelly, are there every month. Rocky has been coming for a few years and it is always lovely to see him, but Andy only started attending more recently and I couldn't believe it when he walked in there. One of the first things we did when we saw each other was have a good laugh about the time I took his blasted nose off when we were sparring and, believe me, I reckon Andy Till is as tough now as he was back then!

I have to admit that I have lived it up quite a bit since I became a member of LEBA, because it is like they say. Quite often, it is not *what* you know but *who* you know. One of the guys I have got to know very well at the meetings is Bob Edgeworth, who I had always known as one of the top timekeepers for the British Boxing Board of Control, but what I never knew was that Bob worked with the England and Wales Cricket Board. When Bob realised how much I loved cricket and how I used to play a lot of cricket, he started to take me to the Oval and Lord's cricket grounds. Because Bob was so well connected, we would get looked after very well and all we would do is just drink Guinness.

There was one time when me and Bob had been drinking some Guinness and then we went out to watch the game. Bob turned around to me and he said, 'James, Alastair Cook is not playing well. Do you think they would notice any difference if we send *you* in?' So I said, 'You know what, Bob? Alastair Cook ain't making much runs. I think I might as *well* go in. You are right. They will *never* know the difference.' There happened to be this bloke sitting in front of us and he was obviously listening to our conversation, but he didn't understand what Bob was getting at, because obviously Alastair Cook is white and I am black. The fella looked at me and he asked Bob, 'What do you mean, they will never know the difference?' So Bob said to him, 'It's all right, his name is James Cook. That is why, if Alastair Cook don't make no runs, we'll send James out there.' I don't think the fella really got the joke, but me and Bob were in stitches.

The LEBA committee are always inviting me to the types of places I could never afford to be if it wasn't for them. Sometimes, you get invited out to places, but nobody cares how you get there and how you get home. But the secretary, Ray Caulfield, always makes sure that I am okay to get there. Ray always makes sure that me and the boys are all right. I must have had dinner at all the top hotels in London, attending amateur boxing shows in beautiful rooms with high ceilings and big chandeliers. I never drank wine before in my life, but I reckon I am a bit of an expert these days. At least I know the difference between red wine and white wine now anyway!

Every year, LEBA holds a fantastic awards lunch at the Connaught Rooms in Great Queen Street. It is always a very special occasion and it is not only members of the organisation who receive the awards. Boxers and trainers from all over the country are honoured, and they all tend to turn up personally to collect their trophies. It is a big room and there is never an empty seat in the place, and there are always loads of really famous faces about. But, just like a Sunday morning meeting, the atmosphere is very laid back, with everybody just mingling and nobody standing on ceremony. We are all there together because of the love of the people around us and it is part of who we are.

I am very proud of the fact that, these days, I have my very own table at the awards lunch. The usual suspects with me are Derek Williams, Sylvester Mittee, Ian Napa, Colin McMillan, Jason Matthews, Prince Rodney and Maurice Hope. A few years ago, me and Derek Williams were going to the awards lunch and Derek was doing the driving. Derek has got this big old Jag and he bloody drives like Miss Daisy! Instead of going 20 miles an hour, Derek will go ten and, if it says ten miles an hour, Derek will go five. That is what Derek is like. Anyway, we were coming from King's Cross and I was telling him where to go, but he was telling me, 'No, it's not that way.' So me and Derek started arguing. I was telling him that I used to drive around the West End all the time, and Derek was ignoring me and he just carried on driving slow. All of a sudden, Derek stopped the car in the road and he said, 'Do you want to have a fight about it?' So I said, 'Yes, we will fight right here and now if you don't go *this* way. *This* is the way to go.' In the end, we went my way, and we even managed to find a great parking space when we arrived.

A couple of hours later, the awards ceremony was in full swing and I was sitting at my table surrounded by friends when, all of a sudden, I got the shock of my bloody life! They only went and called my damn name out to go up on to the stage and collect an award. I swear to God, I had absolutely no idea that that was going to happen. Everybody turned around to look at me and they all started clapping and, as I stood up and walked towards the stage, it took me right back to the first time that I ever came to Stepney Green when they called me up to speak.

They got Billy Schwer to present me with a lovely little statue of a boxer on a wooden plinth, and it has an engraved brass plate saying that it is for dedicated service and support to the members of the London Ex Boxers Association over many years. I managed to say a few words of thanks over the microphone and, by the time I made it back to my table, I was close to tears. I hate getting emotional in front of other people, but I couldn't help it that day. Then, just when I thought I might actually start to cry, good old Mickey Hayes saved the day. He plonked himself down at our table and he started to make everybody's raffle tickets disappear. Poor old Jason Matthews had never met Mickey before and, when Mickey said to him, 'Sorry, son, that's it, they are gone for good now,' you should have seen the look on Jason's face. He was going, 'Hang on a minute, mate, I just paid a tenner for them!' We were all laughing so much.

The London Ex Boxers Association are always helping somebody in one way or another. If the committee are made aware that one of our fellow boxers is in some sort of difficulty, they will always try to do something to assist, although they never make a big deal about that. So many of the members of LEBA put themselves out to turn up and support anything that I happen to be doing to raise funds for the Pedro Club, particularly the boxing shows. In fact, when we were building the boxing gym and we needed some new windows, the chairman, Charlie Wright, went over to see Clapton Glazing on our behalf and he persuaded them to give us such a brilliant deal that we did all the windows in the club.

I remember one day when I went to the LEBA meeting and, at that time, I didn't have enough money to insure the club minibus. A man named Paul Fairweather called me over and gave me £400 that very Sunday. The same day, Stephen Powell's wife, Jill, rang me up and said to me, 'James, I've done a collection for you,' and she gave me over £200. Then, on the Monday, another one of our members, called Tom Burling, who has a building firm, was working at a house around the corner from my place, and Tom dropped me off a cheque. So, therefore, I could afford to insure the minibus that Tuesday with the donations that these guys gave me.

There was another time when Stephen Powell said to me, 'James, I've been speaking to someone to try and get you a donation for the Pedro.' He said they were talking about giving us £500, but Stephen kept speaking to them and, last year, they gave me a donation of £5,000. It is amazing how many members come up to me at the meetings and slip me a cheque or an envelope with some cash in it on the quiet. So these guys are looking out for me very well and I thank them all from the bottom of my heart for that because, without these guys, believe me, the club wouldn't be able to survive.

When I first started attending the meetings, they used to say that I was young blood. Obviously, I am 60 years old now, so they don't call me young blood no more. Everyone gets older, and we have several members in their seventies, eighties and even nineties. So, if we hold a meeting and there is no minute's silence at the start, we always have a round of applause to celebrate the fact that everybody is still with us.

My old friend who was the first one to welcome me to LEBA, Bob Paget, passed away a few years ago because he had cancer, although he put up one hell of a fight. Me, Mel and Sylvester went to visit him in hospital the day before he died. Bob was a very special guy who did so much during his life to help so many people, including the three of us in various different ways. We stayed with him in that little room for about an hour and he was so ill, but I think he knew that we were there. The most important thing was that all three of us had the time to tell Bob what he had meant to us in our lives, and I was so glad that we went. When they held the minute's silence for Bob at the meeting after he left us, you could feel the love in that room was so strong.

That is the only hard thing about being a member of LEBA, when one of our own is taken away from us. But the beautiful thing about it is the way the organisation evolves. We get new guys coming in all the time and we have also got some of the younger fighters who are still active joining us now, and they mix so well with the old guard. I mean, these are young men at the top of their game and bursting with youth, but they always have time to listen to all the stories that the old boys have to tell.

When you are with these guys at the London Ex Boxers Association, it's like being with family, because we all know how hard it is to be a fighter and we are all in it together. The atmosphere in the place is very beautiful, and there is so much wisdom in that room, so much history and so much spirit. Most of the time, when the meeting is closed and the bar is opened, we spend time talking about our memories or just having a laugh, but there is always somebody there to give you advice if you need it.

When I think about what Herol 'Bomber' Graham has been through recently, I really appreciate the fact that these guys at LEBA help to keep me sane and they also keep me on a level where I am no bigger than anybody else. But, at the same time, these guys have made me more famous now than I ever was when I was bloody fighting! Since that first meeting I ever attended, I have come such a long way in so many aspects of my life, and I believe that is largely down to my membership of the London Ex Boxers Association. At LEBA, we have a very simple motto. On the banner that runs across the front of the stage, it says in great big letters, 'It's nice to belong'. I think that says it all.

THE SECRET MILLIONAIRE

ONE day back in early 2006, I received a phone call from somebody at Channel 4. They told me they wanted to make a reality TV show, and they wanted to send this young man to the Pedro Club for me to show him the ropes of being a youth worker, with the camera following us about. To be honest, the first time they approached me, I said, 'No, I am too busy.'

A little while later, they rang me up again. The second time they phoned me, they were telling me a little bit more about this young man they wanted to send to the club, and they said to me, 'He's from Devon.' Devon was where my old amateur trainer, Ronnie White, came from. So I got thinking about how Ronnie took me down there back in the Seventies and I remembered that it was a very beautiful place. I was thinking to myself, 'Who would want to come from a place like Devon to move into London and be a youth worker?' That was when I decided that I would like to meet this young man after all, so I said to them, 'Yes, okay, let him come to us.'

The young man they sent to the Pedro was a fella named Ben Way and, as soon as I met Ben, I thought he was all right. Although he was a posh sort of guy, Ben was down to earth. He never looked down on nobody. He was just normal, doing things his own way. Usually, I can sense it if people are not genuine, and Ben was a genuine guy all the way. He fitted in very well with the kids more or less straightaway, and he never had any problems rolling along with the young people. He got on well with Ufu and he was more than ready to do everything that Ufu asked of him.

To be honest, the first time I began to wonder about Ben a little bit was when we had a management meeting, and he suddenly started to ask all these serious questions. The sort of things he was coming out with made him sound more like an accomplished businessman than a young fella who wanted to get into youth work, and he sounded so confident. I think Ben must have realised that I was watching him closely because, all of a sudden, he went quiet and I didn't really think anything more about it.

The cameras were following us around all the time, and I just thought that that was part of what they were doing. I had no problem with it, because it was in the summertime and I was feeling okay walking around in my black string vest, and I thought they were making me look good! One day, they filmed me and Ben in the ring sparring, and that was very funny. That was my idea actually because I thought it would be a bit of a laugh. At first, the TV people didn't want it. They said we would have to get some kind of clearance, because I think they were scared of health and safety and all this stuff. But I told them, 'Don't worry. I won't hit him. I know what I'm doing.'

Anyway, we put Ben in a headguard and a protector. We both put on a pair of gloves and we got in the ring, and I have got to say that young Ben had plenty of bottle. There was this little man who had never done no boxing in his damn life wanting to come in there and take me out, especially when I started teasing him,tapping him on the head. That was a habit I will always have from when I was fighting. Sometimes, it was just me relaxing. Sometimes, when I knew that people were trying to hurt me, because I had the height, I would just drop my fist down like a brick on their head. It was my way of saying, 'Don't try no crap. I've got you. I am treating you like you are just a little boy.' I remember I used to do that move with Robert Smith all the time when he came to spar with me at Harry Holland's gym because Robert was so much shorter than I was, and he used to hate it! So it was sort of nice to be able to practice that move on Ben, although I obviously never put any power into it.

We moved around in the ring for two minutes and Ben couldn't believe how fast I was, bless him. When it was over, he collapsed flat on to his back and, as I took his hand and pulled him up, I told him never to challenge an old boy who has retired gracefully. Afterwards, they said it was me who gave Ben a black eye. But, just for insurance reasons, I would just like to put it in writing that it wasn't me. I didn't touch him!

Every summer, I like to take Carmen and the girls off to Margate for a little family outing and it happened to be the case that Ben was with us at that time of the year, so we decided to take him down to the coast with us, just to give him a day out. After we had been to the funfair, we all went for a meal. Ben was really shocked when Carmen told him that we had been engaged for 19 years, but that we had never been able to afford to get married. So I told him I wasn't going to get married until I had retired from boxing, and that I was still thinking about making a comeback!

On the last day of filming, I honestly believed that Ben was coming to the house to see me and my family just to say goodbye, so I had a bit of a shock when I answered the front door and he was standing there in this really sharp suit. Before that, I had only ever seen him in casual clothes, and he looked so smart. I said to him, 'Oh, they've given you a new suit now, have they?' He walked into the kitchen and he sat down, and he started to tell us who he really was, that he was really a multi-millionaire and he had come on the show to find a worthy cause to donate his money.

It is very rare that people can completely shock me, but Ben really blew me away that day. Then, right after he broke the news, he gave me another blasted bombshell. He told us that he was giving me and Carmen £10,000 so that we could get married. Carmen was so happy that she started crying, which is a kind of reaction I had never seen from her before. The girls were all so excited. I could tell they were thinking to themselves, 'That's it. Dad can't get away with it no more.

There are going to be no more excuses now!' Everyone was over the moon. As for me, I just sat there with my mouth open in a state of shock. In the end, I said to Ben, 'Okay, I will get married if you will be my best man.'

A few minutes later, Ufu walked in through the kitchen door and told me that Ben had decided to donate £20,000 to the Pedro Club so that we could build a recording studio, and that was enough to make *me* cry because it was something we had wanted to do for a long time. So Ben ended up having both myself and Carmen in tears that day, and Ufu was crying as well, but we were all crying in a good way, if you know what I mean.

Me and Carmen got married a few months later, and it was a beautiful wedding, I must admit. In the past, when I have watched other men wearing white suits to their weddings, I have always wondered why they would want to get married in white because black is my favourite colour. Most of my clothes are black. But, on the day I had to go and pick out the suit that I was going to wear, I don't know why but I tried one on that was kind of ivory coloured and I decided I liked it. Carmen's dress was the same colour and I thought, 'Hell, why not?' Everybody said we both looked great anyway.

There were a good couple of hundred people at our wedding. It was standing room only in the church and, for the reception afterwards, Carmen and her sisters worked so hard to make sure that the day was something really special. Between them, they took care of booking the hall, sorting out the food, the wedding cake and the decorations, which was just as well because, when it comes to ladies' stuff, I don't tend to do a lot. After the meal and before the dancing started, Ben made his best man's speech, and I have to say that it was perfect, especially because he hadn't known me for long enough to say anything embarrassing!

Funnily enough, they put the programme on the telly at the same time Robert Smith of the Boxing Board of Control was flying over to America. He turned on the TV and the first thing Robert saw was my face on the screen. He got such a shock that he thought somebody was playing some kind of joke on him. So Robert immediately jumped up out of his seat and started to look around the plane because he thought somebody was pissing him about. The next time I saw Robert Smith, he said, 'James, I couldn't fucking *believe* it. I was going to America, I turned on the TV on the plane, and guess who was the first face that I saw? It was *your* bloody face.'

Ben Way ended up staying with the Pedro for quite a while. The recording studio that he enabled us to build is still going strong, and that will always be his legacy to us. I believe Ben is living in San Francisco these days, and all I can say is I wish him all the very best in everything he decides to do in the future. Also I am very proud to say that, so I am told, our episode of *The Secret Millionaire* remains the most watched of the whole series.

FROM RICE AND PEAS TO YOUR MAJESTY, PLEASE

ONE morning in 2007, I received a letter through the post that looked sort of official. At first, I didn't take a lot of notice of it, to be honest. It was talking about 'servants' and all of this stuff, and I was thinking, 'What is this? I have never had a bloody servant in my life!' So I just chucked the letter down somewhere and forgot all about it. Then a second letter came through the post, and this time I read it a bit more carefully and I saw that it had 'Downing Street' written on it and it said something about youth justice in Hackney. At the time, I just thought to myself, 'I wonder what this is all about?' It had a little box on the letter they wanted me to tick, so I just ticked the box and sent it back in the envelope they sent me. But, to tell you the truth, I still really had no idea what it was all about.

I never thought about it again until the day the Birthday Honours List came out. My brother, Simon, phoned me because he is a computer whizz-kid and had looked it up on the internet. He said to me, 'Do I have to call you "sir" now?' I said, 'Simon, what are you bloody talking about?' So he said to me, 'James, you are going to see the Queen. She is going to give you the MBE.' So I shot over the road to the shop and asked them to check in the paper to see if my name was on the list, and it was. Then they all started bloody screaming in the shop. But, even when I saw my name on that list in black and white, I was still thinking, 'Is it real? Is it true? Have they made a mistake? It might be another James Cook. They might have the wrong James Cook.'

Soon after that, I got a phone call from the *Hackney Gazette*. The reporter asked, 'Do you know who nominated you?' I said, 'Well, it's definitely not the young people. But I keep telling them they need God in their lives, so maybe it was somebody from the church!' Then the British Boxing Board of Control phoned me up, and then Colin Hart from *The Sun* phoned me. That is when it finally began to sink in that it was actually true. I really was going to Buckingham Palace to meet the Queen.

Growing up in Jamaica, we used to hear all about how the Queen is in charge of the land and how she is a very important lady. When I came to live in the same country as the Queen, as far as I was concerned the Queen might as well have been living on a different planet to me. I thought the Queen would never speak to a black man from Peckham. I thought that, if you meet the Queen, you have got to be royalty or something. Leading up to the time when I was going to meet the Queen, I was joking with people and saying that I would present her with one of my string vests that I like to wear in the summer. But, as the weeks went by, every time I thought about it, I got very nervous.

I hired a formal suit with tails to wear on the day. There was no point in buying one because I would never bloody wear it again. Carmen, Lisa and my sister, Lydia, came with me and I drove us over to the Palace in my car. They sent me through a permit with a seal on it that told me where to park, and I have to say it was a very nice feeling to be driving into the palace with that seal on my old car.

I can see why they call it Buckingham Palace. I would happily live there free of charge. The first thing that caught my eye was the niceness of the palace and how clean it was. I kept thinking about how often they must have to clean it, because everything was very shiny. I think they must just go around and around cleaning it constantly because, by the time they finish, it must be time to start at the beginning all over again.

When you go into the palace, there are things that you don't see every day. When you see the beauty of it, it takes your breath away — the ceiling, the ornaments, the carpets and there was this bloody massive crystal chandelier. I was looking up at it and I was thinking to myself, 'How the bloody hell did they get that up there?' I was looking at these guardsmen standing up straight and they were all so still. I was walking past these fellas and I honestly could not take my eyes off them, because I was thinking to myself, 'Are they real or are they statues?' The way these guys stand up and don't move a muscle for hours and hours, that must seriously take some doing. They are amazing. I found myself wanting to reach out and touch them.

They take you through into this room where you all sit down and have a cup of tea, and then somebody comes and shows you how to greet the Queen and how to reverse away from her afterwards, because nobody is allowed to turn their back on the Queen. But that was fine with me, because I had done enough running backwards, like Muhammad Ali, over the years anyway. Ryan Giggs was in the room with us because he was getting his OBE on the same day, and Manchester United had recently beaten Arsenal. So I went over to shake his hand and I told him, 'I am an Arsenal man,' and he just smiled. We were still shaking hands at the time, so I looked him in the eyes and gave him a smile of my own, and I squeezed his hand a little bit tight, just for a second.

When I saw the Queen in real life for the first time, I was looking at her and I was thinking what a beautiful lady she must have been when she was younger. In fact, I think she is still beautiful now. I could easily see why Prince Philip never did anything bloody stupid! I will be very honest and say that the Queen damn well *frightened* me! Nobody had ever done that to me before. She started to ask me questions, and I actually had to say to her, 'Please, Ma'am, don't ask me no more questions,' because I was so nervous. I was sweating buckets. She told me, 'Hackney needs somebody like you. Keep it up.' So I says, 'Yes, Ma'am,' and then I reversed away from her.

One of the things that impressed me so much was there were probably at least 60 of us in that room and, when you think about the age of the Queen, her memory must be absolutely bloody fantastic. She had obviously learned a little bit about each and every one of us so that she could talk to us in a knowledgeable way, and she had time for everybody. The Queen might be very tiny, but she is so strong. Even though I had been so frightened about meeting her, as I was driving the girls home from Buckingham Palace that day, I just couldn't wipe the bloody smile off my face. Then, in the evening, we had a lovely family celebration at a restaurant and it was all beautiful.

A couple of weeks later, I was invited back to the palace to attend a royal garden party and I saw the Queen again. That was a lovely day, and I had my cup of tea and a few cakes. A couple of months later, I was presented with an award from the British Boxing Board of Control, and then the Boxing Writers' Club gave me another award before the year was out. So 2007 was a truly magical year and I never thought that all of these wonderful things would happen to somebody like me.

Since I was made an MBE, my life has definitely become a lot busier. It is surprising how many people want to start getting in touch when you have letters after your name. These days, it is not unusual for me to receive over 150 messages in one day, and I have to go through them all because some of them are important. I had never carried a diary around before. I would always remember dates in my head, but I have got so many arrangements to keep now that I have got to write everything down. But that is okay, and I just about manage to keep on top of it all. At the end of the day, I have only got one pair of hands, so I just do the best I can.

FROM RICE AND PEAS TO YOUR MAJESTY, PLEASE

There are two of us now who grew up on the North Peckham Estate who have been made an MBE. My friend, Cheryl Sealey, has just received one for her work within her local community. The pair of us might have grown up in a place that people used to say was bad and full of danger, but we still had that love in our hearts. So it just goes to show that it doesn't matter where you come from. Everybody is capable of achieving something good if they have the right attitude, not to hate people, but to try and help people.

Having the MBE has definitely made me very proud, but it is not something that I really think about too much. Sometimes I actually forget about it. I am the same man as I have always been, and I always will be. At least I know I am safe from all of this *Windrush* nonsense now. At least I don't need a passport to prove I am British. If ever those fools decide to come knocking on *my* door, I will just tell them to go and have a word with my very special friend, Her Majesty the Queen!

THE POLICE

THE first time I ever got locked up in a police cell was when I was about 15 years old. I had gone to the Elephant & Castle shopping centre to buy a birthday present for the girlfriend I was seeing at the time, and I was wearing some new school trousers that my mum had got for me. It turned out that a boy from the same school as me, who was wearing the same coloured trousers, had robbed something and this policeman came and grabbed me because he reckoned that I fitted the description. He looked at the present I had bought and he asked me, 'Did you pay for that?' So I says, 'Yeah.' Then he looked at me and he said, 'You are supposed to be in school.'

They took me to Walworth Road Police Station, which was supposed to be a police station that had a very bad reputation at the time, and they put me inside a cell for a couple of hours until my mum came to get me at five o'clock. When they opened the cell door and I heard my mum's voice, I shot out of that door straight past my mum and the policeman. Don't ask me how, but I managed to run right out of the police station, along Camberwell Green, past our favourite Kentucky Fried

THE POLICE

Chicken shop, and I don't think I stopped running until I got all the way home. I knew mum would be shouting and making a noise, so I thought I would let her get upset by herself and get it out of her system a little bit before I had to face her. When I got home, my dad was standing at the front door, but he didn't say anything. So I just ran right past him, straight up the stairs, and I dived underneath the bed. I knew that mum had to go to work so that, when she eventually did get back, she couldn't stay around for too long. I was hiding under that bed thinking to myself, 'I hope I'm going to be safe here for a while,' and I have to say that mum wasn't too bad when she got home.

Back in them times, to be quite honest, the general idea on the street was that the police were not to be trusted. Having said that, there were definitely some good policemen about. I was very sad when, during the time I was running the youth club in Dulwich, this police officer who used to come to the club got killed. He got stabbed in the street just down the road from the club. He used to come in and play cards with us and we used to teach him dominoes. He was such a nice guy, and he was only doing his job. But he was just one man and most of the police offers we came across were not as friendly as he was.

When I was growing up, I remember the 'sus' law very well, which meant 'suspected person' and gave the police the power to stop and search us whenever they wanted to. You would see a lot more black people getting picked on by the police than you do nowadays, in the sense that you could be walking down the road just minding your own business and you could still get stopped. If they saw a black man driving a decent car, they might get him to pull over just to do a random check on his vehicle.

It was a different time back then in many ways. At the end of the day, they were the police and they were the ones who had control. But I think we just accepted it. Back then, if we were driving along the road or walking from Hackney or Peckham to the other side of town, we would probably be hoping that we wouldn't get stopped. Every time you came out of your house, you would probably expect that you might get stopped or pulled up. If there was a whole weekend when we didn't get stopped, I think we would probably celebrate. That is just how things were, but we never let it bother us then and, when I think back to those days, it still doesn't bother me now. You can't hold on to these feelings because, if you do that, you will never move on. You have to let these things go.

One of the things I used to really like was when we were boxing in the amateurs for London or England, and the gym we used to train at was in Westminster Police Station, right near the bridge. So it was sort of a pleasure to be able to walk into a police station and know that the police couldn't do anything to trouble you, because you were going to the gym because you were boxing for London and for your country.

I will never forget one time when there was a competition between the London boxing squad and the police amateur team. I was on my way over there in my car when a policeman pulled me up because I think one of my lights was out. Because of this, I turned up to the show a little bit late. When I walked into the changing room, one of my mates asked me where I had been and I said, 'This bloody policeman just pulled me up, but at least I can beat one of them up tonight without any problem and nobody can say nothing to me about it.' I thought I was going to get my own back. But what I had forgotten was that there was a curtain that sort of separated the two teams, and I didn't realise that the particular policeman I was supposed to be boxing that night was actually on the other side of the curtain and he was listening to me saying what I was going to do and what I wasn't going to do. So, when it came to our fight, he bloody pulled out! I was so disappointed because I had been saying to my mates, 'This is the first time I can hit a policeman and it's legal!'

I was getting ready for one of the ABA finals against Johnny Graham when the first Brixton riot kicked off. I didn't really get involved. But, like everybody else at that time, I went over there to have a look basically to see what was going on. There was a lot of unrest in the air because there had been a big house fire at a 21st birthday party in New Cross Road where 13 young black people lost their lives. The National Front were very big in the area at the time and there was a lot of suspicion about how the fire had started. So a lot of people still believe it was the New Cross Road house fire that tipped the local black population over the edge and made the riots into something much bigger. The scary thing was we knew the family whose house it was where the party was taking place and I had actually been invited to the party. I think I was boxing the following Monday and that was the only reason I never went, so I have got to say that boxing might well have saved my life on that occasion.

Whenever you got stopped by the police, the way they used to act was as if it was their right and that was the end of it. I will never forget the time when I had just won the British title. I was driving through the Rotherhithe Tunnel heading for an early training session and I had noticed that a police car had been following me all the way from Mile End. They eventually stopped me at Jamaica Road and this policeman says to me, 'Where are you going so early?' I told him that I was driving to the gym, and he asked me, 'What is in your boot?' They had been following me for so long and, when the officer asked me to open my boot, I knew that he was thinking bad things. So I asked him, 'What have you stopped me for? Is it for drugs or for speeding?' He said 'Speeding, but we want you to open the boot.'

They searched the car, and they obviously didn't find anything because there was nothing there to find, but they still did me for speeding. The thing was I didn't think that I *had* been speeding. I thought that they just did it out of spite, so I said, 'Okay, we will go to court then.'

I ended up appearing at Mile End Court and, while I was sitting there waiting for my case to come up, I saw a policeman who I knew well because he was an inspector on the British Boxing Board of Control. He was so surprised to see me and he said to me, 'James, what are you doing here?' So I said, 'One of your boys pulled me in.' So he said, 'Does he know who you are?' So I said, 'No.' I remember that he shook his head sadly

THE POLICE

and I will never forget that man's words. He said, 'They don't make it easy for us, do they?'

You see, the thing was the nice policeman knew that I was British champion and it wasn't like me to make trouble, but they had to stop me to pick me up for something that I either didn't do or I didn't have. I think that policeman knew damn well what was going on, and he wasn't happy about it. But, like I said, the times were different in those days. I ended up getting fined 50 quid and they gave me three points on my licence, but then the judge said, 'Mr Cook, forget the fine, but keep the points.' I think even the judge knew that the damn officer had been lying.

A couple of weeks after I got pulled over, I was coming through the same tunnel and another bloody policeman pulled me over. This time, I knew that one of my front lights definitely wasn't working, so I parked the car a bit further away and I thought I would get out of the car and walk back to him quick. So I walked up to him and I said, 'Yes, officer?' He said to me, 'James Cook, can I have your autograph?' I was so happy, because I had thought that he was going to pull me over because of the damn light! So he gave me something to sign, I gave him my autograph, and I was on my way. I got stopped a couple more times after that, but it was never a really big deal and nobody ever wanted to rough me up.

About ten years ago, I am sorry to say that I saw the inside of another police cell. One of my nephews, Jonathan, was driving around in this car and I said to him, 'Where did you get that car from? Show me your licence.' He couldn't show me a licence, so I took the car away from him. I said to him, 'When you show me a licence, you can have the car back.' The next day, me and Keisha drove the car to Tesco and, while Keisha went inside to do a little bit of shopping, I was waiting inside the car in the car park.

Suddenly, I saw these wheel-clamper fellas putting their clamps on this little old lady's car. The old lady was crying, and that got my back up straightaway because I can't stand bullies. But I sort of stayed quiet because I knew that I had an outstanding parking ticket on my car. What I had forgotten was that I was not actually in my own car. On top of that, this car I had taken off my nephew had all these outstanding parking fines registered against it that I didn't know anything about.

The next thing I knew, the clampers had pulled up beside me and one of them said, 'You've got an outstanding parking ticket.' I said, 'Yes, I know, but I only got it on Monday and I've got 14 days to pay, so I am going to pay it on Saturday.' So the wheel-clamper said, 'No, we want it today.' I thought he was being a bit aggressive, but I tried to stay cool. I asked, 'How much is it?' So he says, '£490.' So I says, 'Fuck off!'

Both of them came to the front of the car, and one of them put his hand in and took the keys out of the ignition. So I got out of the car and he decided that he didn't want to give me the keys back, so we started to fight. I hit him once, and then I sort of leaned him up against the car. Then I ran around the car and I hit the other one as well. I ran back to the first one and I was just about to hit him again when I heard a big voice shouting, 'No!' I turned around and there was a policeman

THE POLICE

coming up behind me. Anyway, I was arrested and, funnily enough, a man who I know very well named Tony Cesay, who was a world champion amateur welterweight and is now a great boxing trainer, happened to be walking past at that very moment. Tony actually said to the police officers, 'You lot must have upset him, because James Cook ain't like that,' and Tony was 100 per cent right because I'm normally placid, like my dad used to be.

The police van turned up, and they put me in the back and took me down to the station. The lady at the desk said something about 'M1' and I said, 'You've only just brought me here and now you are going to take me somewhere else down the M1. Why do you want to take me down the motorway?' So the lady said, 'No, M1 is the number of the cell you are going in.' I asked her, 'How long am I going to be here?' She said, 'I haven't got a clue.' Then they put me inside this bloody cell, so I lay down on the bench and I dozed off.

They let Carmen know that I had been arrested, and she was so worried. She got straight on the phone to my cousin, Colin, because Colin works in a solicitor's firm and he knows about the law and how to speak to these people. So Colin got on the phone to the police station pretty damn quick to smooth things out.

There was also the fact that the officers who had come down to the Tesco car park to do the arrest didn't know that I was working with the youth in the area or anything like that, whereas some of the officers at the police station knew about the work I was doing. Either way, I wasn't in that old police cell for too long. In the end, they put me into the van again and they drove me all the way back to the Pedro, so that wasn't so bad.

They used to say that the Pedro Youth Club was a no-go place for the police. But, as far as I was concerned, the police could have always come to the Pedro. In fact, over the years, we have gone out of our way to invite the police into the club. We have had the police in there playing football with the kids and having computer game competitions with them, and anything else I happen to think of that will improve the relationship between the police and the local youth.

There are always about five police officers who come along to the Pedro boxing shows, and a few years ago they spoke to me about working with a thing called the Hackney Independent Advisory Group. Every London borough has one of these advisory groups, which are made up of police officers and ordinary people who represent their local community. The way the police officers explained it to me, it sounded like a very positive thing, so I decided that I would give it a try.

At the advisory group, we all get together about four or five times a year and the meetings are really good, because we bring things up that aren't working and the police are listening to us. If anything is going down in your particular area, you might get a phone call or a text from the police to let you know about it, and they will ask if you can try and calm the situation down. A lot of people, especially the young people, would rather speak to somebody they know before the police come, so we are there to sort of keep the peace.

THE POLICE

When I first joined the advisory group, the man in charge was Detective Chief Superintendent Simon Laurence. Simon was the borough commander of Hackney, and he is definitely one of the good guys. Simon is a man you can talk to properly and you can tell he means the things that he says. Simon has gone off to head up the Grenfell Tower inquiry now. So we miss him, but I think it's great that they have chosen Simon for that job because, if they need an honest person to deal with it, Simon is definitely the right man. The new borough commander is a policewoman called Sue Williams, and the independent advisory group is still going well. I am still as enthusiastic about it as I was when I first joined, but I'm always like that about everything that I do.

The young people around here still get stopped and searched a lot, but I am always telling them not to make themselves so obvious. These young people now are like a different nation. They drive around with their car seats right back and I ask them if the road is up in the sky. They walk about wearing two coats, three hats and four pairs of trousers, and I don't know why they would want to do that. Even when the sun is bloody boiling hot, they are still wearing their blasted woolly hats, so they are definitely going to be drawing attention to themselves.

I suppose, in a way, I can see where they are coming from. When I was a young man, although I never really had too many bad experiences with the police myself, I was listening to everybody else and I was feeding off the negative vibe of other people. But, at the end of the day, the police have got a *hell* of a job to do. Funding-wise, they are in a very bad situation. It is not unusual to have two guns going off on the streets around here in one night and, because of all these cuts the government keeps making, there are nowhere near enough police officers left to be dealing with what they have got to face on a daily basis.

In every walk of life, you are going to get the good, the bad, the ugly and the terrible and, at the end of the day, the police ain't no different. You get good police officers and you get bad ones, and I tell the kids that all the time. To be honest, some of them want to believe it and some of them don't. But realistically, all you can do is tell them the truth and try to get the young people to understand that the police are there for a good reason. The point I always try and get across to the kids is that, God forbid, if something truly bad happens in our lives, like a child going missing or something like that, the first people we turn to are the police.

With memory man himself, Steve Holdsworth, our MC at the Pedro boxing shows.

With John Conteh, Ray Hole and Herol 'Bomber' Graham at the Pedro. John had just done a smashing job raising money for the club with an auction.

Having fun in the sun at a Pedro boxing show with my old mate, and always my hero, Michael Watson.

Former top-class referee, Richie Davies, who is a great supporter of the Pedro Club.

At the London Ex Boxers Association awards lunch with Brian Lawrence, Lenny Lee, Melanie Lloyd and Ian Napa. That is Sylvester Mittee peeping over my right shoulder.

With the chairman of the London Ex Boxers Association, Charlie Wright. We both look like we have halos in this one, only mine is bigger!

Helping Anthony Joshua celebrate his award from the Boxing Writers' Club, with Derek Rowe (photographer) and London Ex Boxers secretary and president, Ray Caulfield and Stephen Powell.

The day the London Ex Boxers presented me with my award. [Philip Sharkey]

Steve Bunce receiving his award from the London Ex Boxers, and look who they got to present it! [Philip Sharkey]

You looking for trouble? With Andy 'Stone Face' Till (aka 'The Mental Milkman') and The Explosive Rocky Kelly.

The three musketeers. With Prince Rodney and Sylvester Mittee.

Enjoying a spot of Sunday lunch with Maurice Hope.

With Detective Chief Superintendent Simon Laurence, the former Borough Commander of Hackney.

At York Hall with Tash and a few kids from the Pedro Youth Club receiving a giant cardboard cheque from Eddie Hearn on behalf of the Matchroom Foundation. [Philip Sharkey]

Taking one of the little ones on the pads out on the local square.

Taking a heavyweight who I am training named Jermaine on the pads. That is the head boxing coach at the Pedro, Tash, in the background.

Tash gloving up one of the local police officers, getting ready to seriously put him through his paces.

These two lads are second generation members of the Pedro. Their mum used to come to the club when she was not much older than they are now.

With my grandson, Keiyon, who is my mini-me. I still say that I am the better looking one out of the pair of us!

The boys on the Ashton on Mersey football team who are being sponsored by NEO Sports Management, a company that I am involved with as a mentor and fitness coach.

James Cook, the businessman at NEO Sports Management. I think I look pretty convincing. [Motion Photo Studios]

Mean, moody and magnificent. [Paul Osman]

Scott Welch, 'The Brighton Rock', comes to the Pedro to see what we've done with his speedball.

A big night out with the lads at the Savoy Hotel. (Left to right: Kevin Mitchell, Lennard Ballack, Jim McDonnell, myself, Michael Watson, Julius Francis, Francis Ampofo, Derek Williams, Colin McMillan and Jason Matthews).

THE SPIRIT OF THE STREET

THEY don't call this area 'the murder mile' no more, but nothing has really changed that much. The truth is that it is still rough around here. There are still the same problems in the area. When the London Olympics came along in 2012, they told us that there would be job opportunities available for people in the local district. They said that the Games would create a lasting legacy of encouraging sports at grassroots level. Out of all the young people I know and come into contact with, I never heard of a single one of them getting a job because of the Olympics. As far as the grassroots sporting legacy is concerned, obviously I don't know what has happened in other parts of the country, but I haven't seen a single damn sign of that around here. As far as I can see, it was all just talk.

One of the latest things the kids are doing now is having block parties. When the block parties first started happening around here and I started hearing about it, at first I didn't know what they were talking about, but I was hearing that a lot of the older people were starting to get upset about the situation. Then, one day, I was on my way to the police station for a meeting with the advisory group and I saw a whole bunch of kids gathering on the corner at the bottom of one of the big blocks of flats. So I stopped and I said to them, 'What is happening here?' They told me, 'James, it's a block party.' So I said, 'What do you mean, a block party?'

They told me that somebody will say on social media that they are having a party outside their block, and then everybody will come down and music will be playing and they will be drinking and dancing, and stuff like that. When I arrived at the meeting in the police station, I brought the subject up. I said, 'People are starting to complain about these block parties now because it is getting very regular.' So the police said, 'Yes, we know about it, James, but we can't really do anything about it. At the moment, all we want to do is make sure that other gangs don't come into the area and cause more problems.'

The thing is, these parties tend to pop up out of nowhere. One night, there was a group of young people gathering down by the end of my block. So I went out there and I walked up to them and said, 'What are you doing?' They told me they were going to have a block party, and I said, 'You ain't having no block party around here. Not on *this* block, you don't.' So they just moved away to another block, and apparently it went on until about bloody two or three o'clock in the morning. So it is no wonder that people are complaining.

When my girls were growing up, I would have gone mad if any one of them had stayed out partying in the street until three o'clock in the morning. But the problem comes from the fact that more than half of the children being raised around the Hackney area grow up in single-parent families. Too many of them have got no strong male role model to look up to and provide any sense of discipline in the home.

When we were growing up, we used to sit down around the table as a family at mealtimes, and that is how you get to learn something about each other. A lot of parents now don't even know what their kids are doing. There are plenty of fast food shops that always seem to be open, and that is all the kids want to eat. So there isn't that quality time now in a lot of families. Families don't really know each other anymore, and I think that is a big part of the problem.

A lot of these kids are following a lifestyle based on what they see all these big pop stars doing in their videos, which are all about drugs, gang warfare and pimping, and all the rubbish that comes along with these things. The only way some of these kids ever see themselves being able to afford the things they want is by selling drugs, and so that is what many of them are aspiring to do.

They can't bank their money, so they have got to spend it and they can't spend it quick enough. They want a big car, so they will be driving around in a new reg car. They pay a fortune for expensive designer clothes, and they might have a bloody £50,000 watch on their wrist. They want champagne. They drink so much champagne when they are out on the street. When we clear up around here after a weekend, the number of empty champagne bottles you see lying about in the road is unbelievable. That is the lifestyle that a lot of these kids are living.

The other thing that you see littered all over the place are these little empty silver bullet-shaped canisters. You see them everywhere nowadays, especially after a block party has gone down. At first, I used to think they were like the alcoholic shot drinks that you get, and I can't tell you how shocked I was to discover that these things are actually full of laughing gas. They are breathing in bloody laughing gas now. The really frightening thing about it is that apparently, if they don't do it right, that stuff can freeze their blasted lungs and they are all inhaling it out of bloody balloons! I was in the park recently in the early morning, and the grass was covered with these things. The sun was bouncing off them, so they were really gleaming. It was as if there was a sea of them. It was like being on the blasted moon!

I grew up in the years when people were helping each other and there was a strong community spirit. In my day, if your neighbour needed help, you helped your neighbour. Nobody wants to help anybody anymore. If they see somebody in trouble, instead of stopping to help or phoning the police for assistance or doing whatever they can do, they just want to record what is going on with their bloody mobile phones and put it on the internet. To me, that is bullshit. You have got to stand up and do the right thing in this life.

Around here, we have got the most diverse community in the world. There are so many different ethnic groups in the area, and they are not mixing together. Everybody is quite happy living by themselves behind their closed doors, when people should be out there supporting each other and helping each other. Too many people are walking around being suspicious instead of getting to know each other and learning about the people who live around them. Next-door neighbours don't even speak to each other anymore.

There is a tenant management organisation based in the local square outside the Pedro. They are a great bunch of people and they are doing everything they can to pull the community together, and we need so much more of that. Sadly, it wasn't so long ago that a young man nearly died a stone's throw away from their office, and it was the same old story. A gang of youths were arguing over nothing, and one of them ended up getting stabbed. Luckily, the ambulance arrived on the scene and they got the lad to hospital in time to save his life.

I am very pleased to say that the tenant management organisation have approached me to work with them. They tell me that they see me as the link to the youth in the area. Last summer, we had a big get-together in the square on a sunny Saturday afternoon. So much work went into putting the day together, and the tenant management team did a marvellous job.

It was all due to start at midday and, by one o'clock, the square was already starting to fill up. We had food stalls selling stuff to eat from all different cultures and an ice cream van and a stall selling punch, because all the nation loves food and drink. We had a bouncy castle and an inflatable Gladiators game for the kids, although a few of the adults couldn't resist having a go on those. We had salsa dancing classes in the centre of the square, and the Pedro football team that had just won the league came along and did a little bit of trickery to entertain the people, which went down very well.

At one end of the square, I organised for there to be a boxing ring for everybody to come in and have a go on the pads with me and Tash. To be honest, I don't think that ring was empty for more than a minute during the whole afternoon. We had everyone in there having a go, from some of the fully fledged boxers from the Pedro Boxing Club having a light workout right down to little girls in pretty summer dresses with their faces painted like fairies and tigers. Derek Williams and Sylvester Mittee turned up, and they were only too ready and willing to give some training tips from the ringside.

The funny thing was that we actually put the boxing ring up at seven o'clock in the morning. I went home and, about an hour later, I looked out of my window to see that some of the local travellers had turned up, and they were getting in the ring to have a spar with each other. I was shouting, 'Oy, get out!' It was all in good fun and everybody was laughing about it, but I decided to stay on guard duty by the ringside for the rest of the morning after that anyway.

A lot of the travellers who live around here come to the Pedro Club, and the parents understand that their kids have got to follow the same rules as all the others. A lot of their kids are coming in to use the boxing club, but it is not only the boxing that they come for. Some of them like to come in for a game of pool or table tennis, and the parents always come across as being very polite.

When I mentioned earlier that I am confident people would protect the Pedro if I ever left the door unlocked, I would include the travellers in that number, without any shadow of a doubt. I would say that the travellers have fitted into the community very well. In fact, I would say they have fitted in much better than a lot of the people around here. You see them out there enjoying themselves and speaking to everybody. I know that travelling people tend to get a lot of bad press, but sometimes I think the rest of us could take a hint from the way they go about their lives.

A couple of the local constabulary came along to the gathering and they stayed for a few hours, standing around and chatting to people. One of them got in the ring to have a go on the pads with Tash, and she didn't half put the poor guy through his paces! It was in the middle of the afternoon and the sun was burning hot, so he must have been sweating like mad underneath all that police gear he was wearing, but it was all good fun.

From a security point of view, there was a community support vehicle parked up at the side of the square for most of the day, and that was cool. They are employed by Hackney Council and they are there to keep us all safe. The van is kitted out with CCTV, and they are the first response for the police and the ambulance service. I would always sooner have them around than not have them around, and the two young men who were operating the van were very pleasant and totally professional.

The whole idea of the day was meant to give the local community a sense of fun and happiness, and I hope that we achieved that. I would say that, in the end, well over 200 people came out to support what we were doing. Every type of person you could find, we had them in the square that day. We had young people, old people, and people from many nationalities and religious backgrounds. Some of the parents who brought their children along used to come to see me at the Pedro Club when they were kids themselves. Carmen's brother, Selvin, was handling the record decks, so there was sweet music playing throughout the day and the atmosphere was really beautiful. It was like a carnival.

Mind you, I felt very bloody tired at the end of it all, and Tash must have felt even more tired than me because she was the one who was doing most of the pad work up in the ring. But it felt great to see boxing being right in the middle of it all. I was so glad that so many people wanted to try it. It felt great to see that in this world that we are living in now, where everything is about health and safety and political correctness, the sport that I grew up in can be out there taking centre stage. So I have to say that the entire day was top notch.

Because I have lived in Hackney for so long and because of my involvement in the way things are around this area, I can't walk down the street without bumping into someone I know. When I am walking around Hackney, I definitely feel like it is very much my manor. All the men want to fist-pump me, and I usually give the ladies a big hug and maybe a little kiss. When I am driving about, I think I must know how the Queen feels sometimes, because I am always waving at people through the window.

In fact, it is not only Hackney that I love. London is my hometown. I am always very comfortable in this beautiful city, and I never have to go very far to bump into someone I know or somebody who remembers me fighting. I think I have just been here for so long now that, if you don't know about me, somebody else will. Basically, I am very proud to be a Londoner.

FINAL REFLECTIONS FROM THE CHAMP

I WAS 47 years old when I returned to Jamaica for the first time. It was unbelievable really because, when I was travelling over there, there were so many people on the plane who I knew. I even bumped into one of my dad's best friends. When we arrived at the place that I used to call home, I swear to God that one of the first things I remember as I was coming up the hill was Carmen's brother, Everoy, standing on top of the roof of their house shouting at me about how I got them all caned by the Teachers Arton on my last day at school before I left for London. All I can say is that it must have been one hell of a caning because it had been nearly 40 years and he had *still* got it in his head!

The next thing I did was go to find my granny's grave and pay my respects to her. While I was standing by the graveside, one of my Uncle Frank's sons came down there. I didn't know if he would remember me, but he knew who I was straightaway and he said, 'Hi, cuz, I heard you was here.'

I think the thing that surprised me more than anything about the Jamaica I returned to was all the changes that had taken place. A lot of the little corner shops that I remembered were still there, but once I got into the town everything was very built up. I was expecting to have to struggle to get to the place where I was born and raised, but there are all these roads now and you can drive straight up to where you want to go, but I think you would still have to have a damn good car to get up some of these steep bloody hills.

My Uncle Frank's place was right on top of the hill, and me and some of the boys decided to take a walk up there to go and see him. The thing was it was so bloody dark, so Carmen said to me, 'I will follow you in the car with the lights so that you can see where you are going.' But I said, 'No, no, I'm with the boys and I am okay.' But Carmen wasn't having it and she followed us anyway, and I was so glad that she did. I mean, I am used to London in the dark, but it was absolutely pitch black. It was like a sort of inky blackness.

When we got to my Uncle Frank's house, my auntie answered the door and I said to her, 'Excuse me, lady, I heard they were selling some land around here.' So my auntie said, 'No, they are not selling no land around here.' I was saying, 'Are you sure? Somebody told me that they were selling land.' My auntie didn't recognise me. Then her daughter came to the door and she said, 'It's Uncle James!' I walked into the house and I said to my Uncle Frank, 'Do you know who I am?' He said, 'Yes, of course I do.' He didn't say nothing much after that. He just stared at me. I don't think he could believe that he was actually seeing me again. When I got back down the hill and back into the light, I was suddenly brave again and I said to Carmen, 'I thought I told you I was okay!' But, deep down, I was thinking, 'Fuck, I am so glad that she *did* follow us with the lights,' because I think I would have probably gone over the gully otherwise.

We stayed over in Jamaica for two weeks, and it was great to see the place again. I have never been back there since, but I will definitely go back another time some day. If I had stayed in Jamaica, I probably would have turned out to be a completely different person to who I am now because it was such a different set-up over there in so many ways. I know that my education probably suffered when I came over to London, but I am not sorry that I didn't turn out to be one of these people who passed ten A-levels. Who knows? If I had never left the country of my birth, I might have gone on to become prime minister, but I wouldn't turn the clock back for all the money in the world. Jamaica is still a very important part of my roots and I will never forget that, but obviously I became British champion and, as far as I am concerned, I am British through and through. Me and Carmen have this argument every day. She keeps telling me to go back to my country!

I am still in touch with many of my friends who I used to run about with on the North Peckham Estate. I saw my old pal Rupert Staple recently. His mum died and I went to the Nine-Night, which is a Jamaican tradition where family and friends gather together to celebrate the life of a loved one who has passed away. The Nine-Night was held on the estate and, when I walked through the place, I saw that it is all chopped up into houses with little gardens now, and it looks so different.

When I think about how well I used to know every nook and cranny of those walkways, if I tried to find my way around the place now, I think it would probably confuse me.

The captain of the Sabina cricket team I used to play for was at the Nine-Night, a man named Milton. At first, I didn't see him, so he grabbed me and he said, 'Jimmy Cook, were you going to walk *past* me?' He told me that the Sabina team was still going strong, which was great to hear. Another good friend who I caught up with at the Nine-Night was Ernest, my old school buddy who advised me to buy my house. I reckon, if I sold that house now, I could probably retire, and it was wonderful to see Ernest again. Ossie Smith wasn't with us because he was in Ghana, but I still see Ossie now and then. Cheryl Sealey would have been there, but she was at a meeting on the same night at New Scotland Yard.

When I asked Melanie to work with me to write this book, I made it clear from the start that I didn't want it to be a book that was just about boxing. But, without the boxing, there would never have been a book in the first place, so there are some things I want to say about the sport I love as Mel and I bring this book up to the finishing line.

When I look back, I am more than happy with what I achieved as a fighter. People sometimes ask me if I earned as much money as Nigel Benn and Chris Eubank. I tell them that I never earned as much money as those two because I never got the opportunity to fight them. I had planned to catch up with them both before I got old, but it never happened. They were busy fighting each other for the WBC and the WBO titles. I was ranked number one in the world at the time by the WBA, but they didn't want to fight me. Ambrose Mendy, who was Nigel Benn's manager, said to me once, 'James, I would never let you fight Nigel because, as a manager, I have got to look after my fighter. If Nigel didn't beat Michael Watson and you beat Michael Watson, how is Nigel going to beat you?'

Now that I have retired from boxing and I am a coach myself, I can see the logic of how Ambrose was thinking, but I still think that it was a shame. I don't have many regrets in boxing or in life, but I have to say that I would have loved to have fought both Nigel and Chris, and I don't just mean because of the money side of it. We were all at the top of our game at the same time and I believe that, if I had fought either one of them, we would have put on an all-time classic. But you can't have everything you want in this world, and the fact is it never happened.

When I think of the aggression and the nastiness that goes on around boxing today, as far as I am concerned, it is just a lot of blasted nonsense. Every boxer knows how tough it is in that ring and, when some of these fighters in the mainstream public eye make all of these horrible threats and they start throwing furniture about, I think it shows a complete lack of respect for the sport of boxing. I know that, in most cases, the needle isn't genuine and they are just trying to build up public interest in the fight, but I don't think you need all of that bloody carry-on to sell a fight. If a fight is there and the people want to see it, they will come out to see it or they will watch it on the telly.

There have been thousands of great fights involving great fighters all the way through, and nobody ever used to crucify each other the way these guys are doing nowadays. I think a lot of them are doing all this trash-talking because they are trying to copy the great Muhammad Ali, but Ali was a one-off. He was clever and he was funny. Some of these guys nowadays look and sound as if they *really* want to kill each other. These guys seem to forget that we all risk our lives every time we step into the ring, and this beautiful sport seriously doesn't deserve to be shown to the world in such a sickening way.

I know that we all have to move along with the times we are living in, but I sometimes think that the boxing fraternity of my generation and those who came before us are like a different species in many ways. You only have to walk into a meeting of the London Ex Boxers Association to see the mutual respect and camaraderie that exists between former fighters, and I only pray that all of the associations in the country continue to survive and flourish so that they can be there for the future generations of fighters coming through.

I always try and keep in touch with as many fighters as I can. Indeed, if I could, I would ring up every fighter I know every day just to say, 'Hello, how are you?' But, even when I bump into the ones I might not have seen or spoken to for a while, we will always stop and speak to each other because we are still part of one big family, and that will always be the case.

Two of the guys I speak to all the time are Ali Forbes and Derek Williams. Us three are like blasted husband and wife. If we don't phone each other, we will text each other. These two guys are like my brothers and there is nothing we wouldn't do for each other. If we don't speak to each other by the end of the week, we are all getting in touch to make sure that everyone is okay. So that is the relationship that the three of us have.

I see Frank Bruno a few times a year. Me and Frank have been friends since our amateur days. We just sort of grew up in different directions because Frank came from Wandsworth and I came from Peckham, not to mention the fact that Frank turned pro with Terry Lawless and I turned pro with Billy Wynter. These days, me and Frank will sometimes phone each other up out of the blue just to check on each other, just to see how each other is doing, and we often speak about many things. I was at a boxing show with Frank recently and the ring announcer made a joke, and the only one in the whole place who laughed was Frank. He went 'Hee, hee, hee' with that laugh of his. Suddenly, everybody started chanting, 'Bruno, Bruno'. It's just that deep, deep voice that he's got, just him alone, and hundreds of people start to laugh. That is the effect the man has on everybody. All the nation loves Frank Bruno.

Scott Welch is another one I have known since the old days. They used to call Scott 'The Brighton Rock'. He was British and Commonwealth heavyweight champion just after the time when I was boxing, and we always used to speak to each other and respect each other. Our friendship sort of grew from there and we often speak on the phone. Scott has done fantastic things for charity. He has climbed mountains and he has done marathons in the desert, and he has raised a lot of money. Scott is head trainer at the Brighton and Hove Boxing Club, and he is always doing stuff for the local youth around his area. He is working with the WBC now to help young people get into boxing, and he recently sent me a WBC speedball for the Pedro boxing gym because we needed a new one.

I always tell people that Michael Watson is my hero because of what he has come through and how he has dealt with it. This is a man they said was brain-dead, and now I can go round his house and make him a cup of tea, and we will sit there for ages telling each other jokes like two old boys. Michael has given so many people so much inspiration. He made an appearance at the Pedro boxing show last summer, and he actually managed to climb into the ring for the first time ever since he was injured. He obviously had to be helped up the steps and through the ropes, but that wasn't too bad. It was the journey back down again afterwards that looked a lot more dicey. But Michael is such a determined man and he took the whole thing in his stride. It was the rest of us who became a little bit emotional.

Sometimes, when the boys are out on the town, Michael and his carer, Lennard Ballack, come out with us. We were all together recently at the Prince Regent Hotel. It was a charity dinner and they were celebrating the British war heroes. On the same table, we also had Jason Matthews, Colin McMillan, Derek Williams, the trainer, Jim McDonnell, and former British and Commonwealth super-featherweight champion, Kevin Mitchell. Good old Francis Ampofo was there too. Francis is a chicken farmer who always brings me eggs for Carmen whenever he comes down from Norwich. This time, Francis forgot to bring the eggs and I said, 'What am I going to tell my missus when I get home?' Then finally, Julius Francis was the last to arrive. Julius also comes from Norwich, and we were actually sitting down at the table eating when he strolled in. I said to him, 'How come you are so late when you only live down the road from Francis, and he has been here for bloody ages?' We were all taking the piss out of Julius, telling him that he was running on black man's time!

I have been retired from boxing for almost a quarter of a century and people still remember me, which is great. The other day, I was driving down Morning Lane in Hackney with the window down, and this bloke shouted out, 'James Cook, good fighter!' I thought, 24 years and they still remember! I was at the Savoy Hotel in the Strand attending the Boxing Writers' Club awards dinner this year and I was sitting next to Billy Schwer. Billy said to me, 'James, do you realise that you and I have been sitting at this very table for this occasion for 27 years?' That really blew me away.

Every fight that you have, you learn something about yourself. You kind of take it in and you put it away. I have learnt so much from boxing, and I am just glad that I am fit and well enough to tell my story. I will say to anybody, 'If you retire from boxing and you speak like me, then you had a good career.' Mind you, when Mel interviewed me for her first *Sweet Fighting Man* book, she asked me how long I had been over here. When I told her, she said, 'You still speak very Jamaican.' So I said to her, 'You should have heard me when I was ten years old. I couldn't even understand myself!'

I have to admit that time has been kind to me in many ways and, as this old boy comes into his sixties, I don't think he is looking too shabby. This lady came over to the Pedro Club the other day and she asked me how long it had been going, and I told her it had been there since 1929. She looked at me with surprise, and I said to her, 'Yeah, the cocoa butter is working really well.'

Obviously, we all start to get a few aches and pains as the years go by, but I still feel young in many ways. But, to be honest, these days, I am becoming like old Uncle Remus. The young people like to sit down and listen to me telling stories. The other night, a young man said to me, 'James, tell me that one again about when you underestimated your opponent and the referee said. "I told you so."' He was talking about Harry Gibbs and the Tony Burke fight. So, they were all gathered around me while I was telling that story because that is one of their favourites.

Another one of my tales that always goes down well with the kids is about the time that I ended up racing sheep with Larry O'Connell and Colin McMillan. Back in the Nineties, they made Larry a freeman of the City of London, and we found out that he was entitled to herd sheep across any bridge in London. So we decided to have a sheep race to raise money for the Angels With Dirty Faces, which was good old Bob Paget's charity that he used to run to help the pensioners of Peckham. They gave us these sheep to race across the Southwark Bridge, and they gave Colin McMillan the fastest sheep because he was lighter than everybody else. Colin started out like Usain Bolt, and I reckon they gave Colin's sheep bloody steroids. But me and my sheep were first over the finish line, and I reckon they gave me the slowest damn sheep that was there! I think the reason the kids like that story so much is because it comes from another world to the one they know. It is a sad thing, but many of these kids have never even *seen* a damn sheep in real life.

A couple of years ago, some friends asked me to help them start a company called NEO Sports Management. One of them is a barrister named Michael Neofytou, who I met back in the day through Frank Maloney, and the other one is a solicitor named Keith Lobo. Michael was the one who started the company and he said to me, 'James, we want to bring you in.' I said, 'But I haven't got any money.' So he said to me, 'Listen, the reason we want to bring you into the company is because we trust you.'

Our aim is to help aspiring sportspeople with things like contracts, finances, sponsorship, legal stuff and handling the media, which obviously Michael and Keith take care of. Where I come in is as a fitness coach and a mentor to our clients. We are also focusing on putting money back into sport at grassroots level. For example, we are sponsoring an under-eights football team called Ashton on Mersey, who are based in Manchester. The company has provided the lads with new kits, tracksuits and some training equipment. So far this season, those boys have won nine games and only lost one, so hopefully there are some little stars of the future amongst them.

One of the biggest highlights of my life has to be meeting the Queen at Buckingham Palace. Although he has never actually admitted it to me, I have always thought that Paul

Fletcher from the Rathbone Foundation was the one who was behind all the work for me to be made an MBE. When I talk to him about it, he just smiles and says, 'It wasn't me.' But I have got a big feeling that it was him. My old Rathbone manager, Aminul Hoque, got the MBE in the next honours list after me. But I got the Queen and he didn't, so I still like to tease him about that. Paul and Aminul are both great guys who take pleasure in helping people, and I loved working with the pair of them.

When I hear on the news or I read in the paper about there being so much unrest between the different cultures all over the country, I honestly don't understand what that is all about. It seems to me that so many people are getting offended by this or offended by that. It is almost as if people are *looking* for something to be offended about. When I think back to my mum and dad's generation and all the stuff they had to go through, I would have thought that, if anybody had reason to get upset, it would be that generation, or even my generation.

People say that the problems are happening because we have got too many different cultures in the country now, but we had all of that back in our day too. It was never just black and white. There were all of the shades in between, and we all got along all right. Of course, there were problems, but back then everything seemed so much more straightforward. Back then, if somebody didn't like you because you were black, they weren't afraid to tell you. These days, things seem to have become so much more complicated.

I was brought up as a Christian, and I definitely believe that God is up there and he is the one who put breath into us. Whenever anything happens that surprises us or shocks us or pleases us, the first thing we say is, 'Oh God!' I was talking to a young man in the Pedro recently whose girlfriend has a baby on the way. He was complaining because he is having to work all the hours that God sends. I told him that, if he is man enough to have a child, then he must be tough enough to put in the hours. I also explained to him that, if God wants you to work around the clock to survive, then he will give you the health and the strength that you need. As my mum always used to say, 'God may be slow, but he is sure.' One thing I have absolutely no doubt about is the fact that somebody or something has been watching over me in a big way, because I have been fortunate enough to have so many wonderful people in my life.

Jimmy Redwell and Ronnie White at the East Lane Boxing Club gave me such a great boxing foundation, and they also made me realise that working with young people was what I really wanted to do. These two men played such a big part in shaping the person I have become in my life, and I will always be very grateful to them both for that.

Carmen's mum and dad were two great people. Whenever I couldn't speak to my own mum and dad, I would either speak to Carmen's parents or I would speak to my Auntie Lovely. She was the rebel of the family and, if I ever went to Auntie Lovely and told her that somebody was giving me a problem, she would probably say, 'Tell them to fuck off.' Carmen's parents would be calm and reasonable. They would say, 'No, James, you don't do it that way. You do it this way.' So I would get advice from every angle.

My dad was such an easy-going father who didn't want any trouble. If I told my dad the police had been following me, he would probably say, 'Well, you must have done something wrong for the policeman to follow you.' That is how bloody placid he was. To get dad upset, you would have to move a bloody mountain or put a stick of dynamite under him. Mum was a different story. My mum would probably say, 'What are they following you for? You would *never* do that.' So mum was the one who would get up and do the fighting, whereas dad would do anything for a quiet life. But dad was out there working hard every single day to make sure his family had a roof over their heads and plenty of food on the table, and he gave us all a good life. Dad is still alive and, these days, he is so funny. When I think about what a docile guy he used to be, I think my dad would probably want to fight you now because he is in his eighties. He was a great dad to have around, and he still is.

We lost mum about ten years ago. To be honest, I think mum knew that she had something very badly wrong with her, but she didn't want to tell us. So, when the doctor said the word 'cancer' to us, we were so frightened. There was four of us, her sons, all rearing up on the doctor and saying, 'What do you mean, cancer? What you need to do is just get her better right now!' The poor doctor was only doing his job, but we weren't thinking straight. In the end, we kind of calmed down. We had to, because otherwise the doctor said that he was going to have to call security.

I still think about my mum almost every day. Even now, whenever I know I have messed up in one way or another, I know that my mum is still there smiling down on me, and she will be saying, 'I *told* you.' All of the things my mum used to say and do, the records she used to play, it all reminds me of her. She was a good mum, and I loved her with all of my heart.

It is hard to put into words how brilliant Carmen has been. She has got such a warm and loving nature and she will give anybody everything. She will leave herself short just to make sure that somebody else has got something. Unless you really know Carmen, you would never know how much she has done for other people because that is the kind of person she is. Carmen's mum was exactly the same, and sometimes I look at Carmen and I say, 'You are just like your bloody mum. You give the world.' Carmen has always stood by me and she has always been there for me, and there is nothing in the world that I wouldn't give her. Life with Carmen just gets better all the time, and we now have six wonderful grandchildren.

I have two grandsons named Keiyon and Jayden, who are both 11 years old. They are the boys who danced in the ring at the Pedro boxing show last year. Keiyon is Keisha's son, and he has just got a part in the TV drama *Top Boy*, which is all about gang life on the London estates. The programme has been taken over by the rapper, Drake, and it is coming out on Netflix. Keiyon knows that it is a huge opportunity for him and he is handling the situation so well, going up to Manchester to film and everything. Mind you, me and Keiyon have problems every day because he tells me, 'Grandad, people say that I look like you, but they say that I am better looking than you.' The thing is that he *does* look a lot like me, but I think I am the better looking out of the pair of us!

Jayden is Patricia's son. Jayden sings very well, he is a good actor and he plays football as well. Jayden is in stage school and, at the moment, he is appearing in the musical show *Motown*, which is on at the Shaftesbury Theatre in the West End. When I think back to when I was the same age as Jayden and all I could afford to do was look in the shop windows around that part of town, it makes me feel so damn proud that a grandson of mine is performing on the stage right in the middle of it all. Jayden wants to learn boxing, whereas Keiyon is more of a comedian. I really admire the way they are both so focused, and they are doing things I never thought or dreamt I would see them doing.

I also have four granddaughters. Tia-Elise is Lisa's daughter and she is like a proper little madam. She is five years old, going on bloody 20. She comes home from school and she goes upstairs to her room to get changed, and I say to her, 'Where are you going? Why are you dressing up like that?' She will say to me, 'Because these are my clothes, grandad.' She is a real little lady, and she is going to drama school as well.

Ella-May is Patricia's daughter. She is nine years old and most of the time she is one of the quietest young ladies you would ever see. She has a beautiful singing voice and the only time she likes to make herself heard is when she is singing while the rest of us are watching the telly. The boys will tell her to be quiet, but I always say, 'Leave her alone and let her sing.'

Janae and Jayla are Jamie's twin girls. They are two and a half years old, and I think I am the only one who can shout at them and they will actually bloody listen. They are running around all over the place now and, as twins, they seem to know all about each other. It is like they are in tune with one another, but they are so identical that I haven't got a clue who is who, to tell you the truth. The other day, I said to Jamie, 'You need to put name tags on them.' When I am calling them, I don't call them by name. I just say, 'Hey, you!' I will be shouting at one of them, and then the other one will probably start doing something and then I will be shouting at that one, saying, 'Hey, you, sit down and don't move!' Jamie will come in and she'll say, 'Which one are you talking to, dad?' I will just randomly point at one of them and say, 'That one!'

I am proud to say that the Cook family name is going from strength to strength in the sporting world. Evans has got three sons out there playing professional football. Two of them started out with Arsenal and one started with Cardiff City, but they all came to realise that, to get a break, sometimes you have got to make a move somewhere else.

There is Anthony Cook, who is a winger for Dulwich Hamlet. There is Regan Evans Charles-Cook, who is a midfielder for Gillingham. Also, there is Reice Charles-Cook, who is a goalkeeper, and it has just been in the paper that Reice needs to learn Danish because he has just left Swindon to sign up with a team in Denmark called SønderjyskE Fodbold, and please don't ever ask me to pronounce that! So all three of them are coming through, which is lovely because, for so many years, I saw Evans and his missus taking them all over the place, week in, week out, and it is great for my brother and his wife that all their hard work and commitment has paid off. Those boys knew what they wanted and they went for it. People think of footballers as being rich and spoilt, but I am proud to say that all three of my nephews are nice guys.

No amount of richness has ever excited me. Right now, I am driving around in an old Lexus that has still got a cassette tape player in it, believe it or not. People always say to me, 'James, what are you doing with that old car?' But I like that car very much and I don't care what anybody says. I know that this side of my nature definitely came from my granny. She was the one who taught me that material things are not important. Somebody would come around to our house in Jamaica, and my granny would always cook up a big pot of food and she would put it down on the table for everybody to share. She used to say to me, 'James, whatever happens, you can't hide food from people.' My granny taught me that what really matters is knowing how to share, how to give and how to love, and I will never, ever forget that.

When I was younger, I never dreamt that my name would be in the papers and I certainly never thought that I would end up having my own book. I understand that I am not going to be around forever and I hope that, when the day comes that

I am not here, somebody else can pick up where I left off and carry on flying the flag for the Pedro Youth Club to make sure it carries on for future generations to come. In the meantime, all I can say is that, as long as I am still on this planet, it is going to be very hard to keep me down.